Army Writing Guide

Army Writing Guide

How to Write NCOERs and Awards

MSG Parker

This information is provided for educational purposes only. Any reference bearing resemblance to real persons, living or dead, is purely coincidental. Although every effort has been made to ensure accuracy, no warranty or guarantee, expressed or implied, as to the accuracy, reliability or completeness of furnished information is provided. The author and publisher are not responsible for damages resulting from the use of this book.

Copyright © 2010 by MSG Parker

All rights reserved

ISBN 9-780-98-4356-317

Published and Designed by Military Writer Press

Printed in the United States of America

No part of this book may be reproduced by any means, whether electronic or mechanical, without the written consent of the publisher.

Dedicated to the men and women serving our country
around the world, far from home and family

Introduction

Victorious warriors win first and then go to war, while defeated warriors go to war first and then seek to win. –Sun Tzu, The Art of War

A variety of changes in Army manning and mission requirements have resulted in unprecedented changes. Opportunities for advancement have never been better. And one of the best ways to benefit from these changing times and help your career is to make sure you turn in quality NCOERs and awards.

NCOERs and awards are the currency of Army advancement. In today's large and impersonal military where the people in charge of promotions have no direct knowledge of your performance or abilities, NCOERs and awards are vitally important to ensure you remain competitive for that next stripe.

The purpose of this book is to aid Soldiers in writing effective NCOERs and awards that will ensure their eligibility for the promotion and career opportunities they've earned.

This book is not an authority on Army administrative practices and requirements and is intended only to serve as a quick reference for phrases and ideas.

This book would not have been possible without the kind and generous contributions and suggestions submitted by visitors to the ArmyWriter.com website. Comments, suggestions, or corrections should be sent to editor@armywriter.com. Any corrections or improvements will be included in this book's next edition.

Army Writing Guide

How to Write an NCOER

An NCOER (DA Form 2166-8) is a form used to document a person's performance for a specific length of time –usually a year. Everyone in the Army has their performance rated and recorded this way and, if you're a supervisor, you'll be responsible for writing NCOERs for the people you report on. The supervisor is responsible for writing the NCOER but it's common for the supervisor to ask the Soldier being rated for material. Some people might call this writing their own NCOER but, in my opinion, it's not. Supervisors who care about their troops want to write the best NCOER possible and may ask the subordinate for information to make sure they didn't miss any notable achievements. It's in the Soldier's best interest to provide as much information as possible.

A well-written NCOER is important and critical to advancement. Promotions are competitive and only those Soldiers who meet or exceed standards of performance will be considered. If your NCOER doesn't accurately describe your performance, your efforts may not be recognized and you may be rated lower than you deserve. Or you may not receive the assignment you're qualified for because your NCOER doesn't completely describe your skills and accomplishments. An accurate NCOER is vital to your career.

And when you consider your career with the Army, think positive. We all go through our ups and downs and sometimes we get discouraged and think, "I won't be promoted so why bother to make an effort?"

Don't fall into this self-defeating trap. You can be promoted! You *will be* promoted. I don't mean to belittle our NCO Corps but I have seen people who could barely speak English or pass a test get promoted –again and again! So I know *you* will be promoted. So why wait? Take action now!

And don't be intimidated by the perceived increase in responsibility. This is not an issue for some people but for most, it is. It might be hard to picture yourself serving at the next rank, performing your supervisor's duties. It may seem as if your supervisor smoothly carries out his or her responsibilities and it might be hard to imagine yourself in the same role. And that's natural because we're all different and we all approach tasks in different ways. The way you execute the duties of your next rank will be different than your predecessor and may even be more efficient.

The first thing that must be understood about NCOERs is that it's not the words or glowing phrases that get you promoted –it's the rating of your supervisor. And that, as you know, depends heavily on your performance during the reporting period. But you already know that and if you bought this book, you're interested in turning whatever performance you *do* have into the best NCOER possible.

And it is possible to write an NCOER in such a way that it will be difficult for your supervisor to grade you as anything less than the highest rating.

The following tutorials take you step by step through the process of developing material for your NCOER and shaping it into the most effective NCOER possible.

Gathering Content for the NCOER

When the annual evaluation comes due, it's often hard to come up with enough accomplishments to fill the blocks. The things we do every day just don't seem out of the ordinary or worthy of an NCOER. But they are. The things that all of us do every day are essential to the continued success of the Army's mission.

The quickest and most effective way to come up with material for your NCOER is to brainstorm first. List all the ratee's accomplishments on a separate sheet of paper. Write down everything that might qualify as a bullet. Nothing is too small or off-limits. Make sure off-duty education, duty qualification, community involvement, and training are addressed.

One thing that's important to note is that when you're putting together a list of accomplishments, don't hold back! If you're new to NCOERs, you might be reluctant to claim credit for any achievements that you weren't 100% responsible for. Don't be! Most work center accomplishments require the efforts of many people and are the product of teamwork. If you had *any* part in an accomplishment, you are allowed to claim it and list it as an accomplishment. A supervisor will often reuse the same accomplishments, over and over, in several different NCOERs so it's not unexpected or unprecedented. As a rule of thumb, if you had any part in an achievement, from documenting it in a log to turning a wrench, you can claim it. So claim everything and let your supervisor sort it out. And don't worry that your supervisor will scrutinize your inputs and dispute your claims. It doesn't happen. A supervisor is much more concerned with getting decent material for your evaluation than with analyzing which person contributed the most to this or that project. He or she will be delighted that you provided anything at all. A lot of people don't provide anything!

Now is no time to be modest. One of the most common hurdles for first-time NCOER writers is modesty. Most of us don't want to appear as if we're bragging about our performance and that's admirable. But when it comes to NCOERs, your goal is to make it sound as if you're the best Soldier ever! In Army evaluations, we always write to make it sound as if we invented the alphabet or developed the internet! We always exaggerate somewhat. That's just the way it's done and you have to get in that mode! When you get used to it, it can actually be kind of fun.

After you've brainstormed and came up with a list of accomplishments, sort them into the categories required by the NCOER form:

- Army Values
- Competence (duty-related, primary or collateral duties)
- Physical Fitness & Military Bearing
- Leadership (mentoring, community service)
- Training (duty qualification, self-improvement)
- Responsibility and Accountability

Don't be surprised if your list of accomplishments doesn't fit neatly into these categories. You'll probably have to reverse-engineer your bullets to fit them into these topics or look for more achievements that fit the required category.

For example, if you're not a supervisor, you may not have any obvious feats of leadership. You'll have to think outside the box and find something that qualifies as a leadership bullet.

Don't have enough or the right type of accomplishments? You can bend the rules a little by signing up for accomplishments at the last minute as long as it's done before the end of the rating period. Normally, because the unit requires the NCOER to be completed months before the end of the reporting period, it's usually possible. Enroll in a college class (your bullet will have to say, "currently enrolled in..." rather than "completed so and so credit hours" but it's better than nothing). Sign up for Habitat for Humanity, volunteer for the next change of command ceremony, etc. Don't let the opportunity to excel slip away. If possible, ask your supervisor to assign a challenging additional duty that you can claim on your evaluation. The best additional duties are those that show advancement. When a board sits down and goes through your records, they will flip through your NCOERs and will expect to see growth and progression year after year. If you were tool monitor last year, this year you should have an additional duty with increased responsibility.

After you've brainstormed and come up with a suitable list of accomplishments and sorted them into the required categories, it's time to reword those bullet comments until they're as descriptive as possible.

But before we go further, we should review the format required for bullet comments.

NCOER Bullet Comment Format

The style of writing required on the NCOER is the bullet comment format. A bullet comment is an abbreviated style of writing. Forget what your teacher taught you about proper grammar and punctuation. In this manner of writing, the accomplishment is listed in short sentence fragments – like this:

o completed over 200 reports in least time ever, maintained 100% accuracy

o his work, sense of responsibility inspired peers, raised shop production rate to best ever

The reason for writing like this is to conserve space. There isn't much room on the NCOER form and this allows fitting in the most information. It also discourages the use of unnecessarily wordy or flowery descriptions and promotes getting straight to the point.

The bullet comment has two main parts: the accomplishment and the result. Normally, the accomplishment is listed first followed by the positive result (shown in bold type below):

o conducted over 100 missions; **maintained a 99% on-time delivery rate**

A bullet comment written without an impact or result will probably be weak and vague. The reader will be left to wonder, "So what if over 100 missions were conducted. Is that more than the norm? What was so special about that?" The impact or result of the action answers that question.

Official Guidance

Note that DA Pamphlet 623-3 specifies the format for bullet comments. Before we go any farther we should review the format specified by DA Pamphlet 623-3 para 3-7:

> *b. Bullet comments.* Bullet comments are mandatory regardless of ratings given. Narrative rules for Part IV, bullet comments will—
>
> (1) be short, concise, to the point. Bullets will not be longer than two lines, preferably one; and no more than one bullet to a line.
>
> (2) Start with action words (verbs) or possessive pronouns (his or her); Personal pronouns he or she may be used; should use 'past' tense when addressing NCO's performance and/or contributions.
>
> (3) Be double-spaced between bullets.
>
> (4) Be preceded by a small letter 'o' to designate the start of the comment. Each bullet comment must start with a small letter unless it's a proper noun that is usually capitalized.

(5) A specific example can be used only once; therefore, the rater must decide under which responsibility the bullet fits best (or is most applicable)

As stated above, bullet comments may begin with a verb or a possessive pronoun (his or her). But in general, most of the time a strong, direct bullet should start with a verb. Only use a pronoun when it's really necessary such as when describing personal characteristics.

Types of Bullet Comments

In order to better understand the nature and anatomy of successful bullet comments, hundreds of bullet statements from a variety of Occupational Specialties were studied and compared. A careful analysis showed that NCOER bullet comments consisted of three main types (or a combination thereof):

- Achievement
- Recognition
- Skill or Character Description

Examples of each type are shown below:

Achievement

o conducted over 200 missions into...

o developed the first-ever SOP that...

o fielded 22 advanced transport systems...

o established successful method for...

o improved section efficiency by 50%...

Recognition

o selected over peers to compete for...

o commended by Commander for...

o awarded Army Achievement Medal for...

o earned commendable rating during...

o received Battalion coin for...

Skill or Character Description

o displayed outstanding battle staff skills

o committed to excellence

o his sound judgment and tactical savvy...

o delegated effectively

o resourceful and innovative...

Achievement-type bullets have the most impact. They describe exactly what was accomplished and the impact of that accomplishment. The best NCOER bullet comments are the Achievement type. If possible, the NCOER should be packed with this type of bullet. The more specific, the better.

Recognition-type bullet comments don't normally list an impact as the recognition itself is considered to be the impact or significant result. This type of bullet, while significant, is vague; they often don't say exactly *why* a person was recognized.

The Skill or Character Description bullets, although very commonly used in NCOERs, are the most unsupported of the three types of bullet comments in that they don't convey specific facts. But, even though they are somewhat unsupported, they are sometimes appropriate and useful. A ratee's character can't be adequately describe with an Achievement-type bullet comment. A Soldier might be the very best at turning out reports or maintaining trucks but might be the absolute worst at sharing information or helping others. And those social traits are important, just as important as technical skill. A Soldier who can't function as a member of a team shouldn't and likely won't be promoted. The Skill or Character-type bullets allow a person's personality and leadership skills to be expressed.

Writing Effective Bullet Comments

After brainstorming and gathering all your accomplishments, start reviewing your material and focus on one bullet at a time.

Step 1. From your list of accomplishments, take your first bullet and rework it so that the bullet begins with a past tense verb:

"Drove over 900 miles..."

Don't add any qualifiers such as "safely drove" or "efficiently drove" –just write the appropriate verb. The effect of the driving will be described in the result portion of the bullet.

Step 2. Describe the positive effect or result of the action described.

"delivered more than 20 tons of critical supplies with zero equipment failures, accidents, or loss of personnel"

Step 3. Put it all together. Every bullet has to communicate what was done and what the result was. That's the basics. Once that is accomplished, go back and make sure that the bullet is accurate and contains all the information pertaining to the achievement. Was the delivery on time? Did the deliveries prevent any disaster or promote success? Is the impact listed the most significant? It's very important to make sure you didn't leave anything out. You don't want to cheat yourself out of a promotion, do you?

"Drove over 900 miles through Iraq's most dangerous quadrant, delivered over 20 tons of critical supplies on time with zero equipment failures, accidents, or loss of personnel"

Try to give yourself as much credit as possible. Give the circumstances surrounding the achievement some thought. Were other people affected? Did less people get lost because of your foresight and planning? Did people benefit? Include those facts! They show responsibility and teamwork!

Perform these steps for each bullet comment. Remember: to be competitive, every bullet statement should describe a result of the action listed.

Each bullet comment should describe something the ratee actually accomplished. Try to avoid general statements like "always chooses the hard right over the easy wrong". That does convey a certain ideal but it's not specific enough for a good NCOER and it's so common that it has no effect.

Do not waste bullet space by re-listing something that's already in your duty description! Many people sabotage their NCOERs by peppering them with statements that lack impact and belong in the duty description. For example:

"o processed award packages, deftly handled office correspondence"

If a Soldier does that, unless he's working outside his specialty, that information should already be in the job description! The NCOER has precious little room available for entries. Make sure it's not wasted.

What sets an NCOER apart from all the other equal score NCOERs? Bullet comments! What would catch your eye? A boring and common "always chooses the hard right over the easy wrong" or a unique and powerful bullet such as "sacrificed his assignment to remain with platoon until replacements arrived"?

Keep in mind that the Army wants well-rounded people. Your NCOER should reflect this; make sure you include bullet statements that represent all the categories required *and* whatever trait the Army is emphasizing at the moment (suicide prevention, sexual harassment, etc).

And try to make sure your bullet comments show an increase in ability and responsibility over what was in your previous NCOER. The goal for Soldiers is growth. When the promotion board flips through your records, they will be looking to see if you progressed year after year. The NCOER, although it can stand alone as a record of performance, is actually only one segment of your overall performance record. If you were Tool Monitor last year, this year you should be in charge of Bench Stock or Supply or some other position that's known to require more knowledge and responsibility.

How to Write Bullet Comments with Impact

Many of us find it difficult to write good bullet comments for our jobs. Getting those reports out on time or driving the bus just doesn't inspire a lot of glory. But, if we take the time to examine how bullet comments are normally constructed, it becomes obvious that writing good bullets is as much the result of using a good algorithm as having good material and that it's possible to make good bullets out of what might be considered to be ordinary accomplishments.

The most vital component of a bullet comment is its impact. Without a good impact or result, a bullet comment is ineffective and doesn't communicate to the reader what was actually accomplished.

After studying hundreds of bullet comments across a variety of occupational specialties, it was determined that, in general, the impact of a bullet comment is traditionally expressed in 9 ways:

Achieved a Quantity. This type of result or impact statement is used when the quantity itself is the significant achievement: number of missions completed, number of insurgents captured, number of miles driven, number of flights supported, etc.

Achieved an Objective. This type of impact description is used when the named objective is universally recognized as being significant and no further explanation is needed: completed successful rotation, finished an inspection, repaired, restored capability, etc.

Reduced an Undesirable Condition. This type of impact statement describes initiative that results in a better condition: a reduction in the number of equipment failures, in the number of incidents of sniper activity, number of late reports or awards, length of time required, etc)

Improved a Condition. This type of result is another way of describing improved conditions or processes: increased readiness, streamlined admission procedures, combined efforts, increased efficiency, etc.

Prevented Undesirable Condition. This type is used to describe proactive efficiency: surveillance prevented IED use, analysis of route prevented threat to personnel, PMCS prevented equipment failure, etc.

Maintained Ops Tempo. This impact type is used to document significant and critical achievement: maintained operational rate of 95%, ensured readiness, maintained 100% accuracy, zero errors, etc.

Comparison to Peers. This method is usually used in Recognition bullet comments and is an effective way of making the ratee standout: qualified 2 months ahead of peers, chosen over others of equal rank, etc.

Timeliness. Achievements related to time use this type of impact statement: completed ahead of schedule, finished before required, no late reports, guaranteed zero delays, etc.

Name Dropping. This type is used when the name of the event specified is universally recognized as being highly significant and so important that it becomes the impact and no further explanation is needed: supported ops in Sunni Triangle, key to the success of OEF III, completed over 100 missions ISO OPERATION ANVIL TREE, etc.

Try applying these nine types of impact to your bullet comment to determine which one works best and is the most significant. The goal is not merely what fits but what works *best* –which type of result is most significant. For example, consider the following comment:

"completed over 120 ops reports with 100% accuracy"

In order to develop and determine which kind of impact statement is most appropriate for this comment, a writer would have to have direct knowledge of the job or achievement but some suggestions are listed below:

"completed over 120 ops reports with 100% accuracy, **exceeded norm for production by 50%**" (Quantity)

"completed over 120 ops reports with 100% accuracy, **reduced unnecessary retransmissions by 50%**" (Reduced undesirable condition)

"completed over 120 ops reports with 100% accuracy, **saved $10K in TDY costs by gathering info by teleconference** " (Prevented undesirable act)

"completed over 120 ops reports with 100% accuracy; **maintained a 99% operational rate despite 50% manning deployed**" (Maintained ops tempo)

"completed over 120 ops reports with 100% accuracy; **best performer in section!**" (Comparison to Peers)

"completed over 120 ops reports with 100% accuracy; **best on-time delivery in 5 years**" (Timeliness) "completed over 120 ops reports with 100% accuracy, **support key to success of OPERATION ANVIL TREE**" (Name Dropping)

The best bullet comment depends on context. If you already have a bullet comment that emphasizes saving the government money, then the best of the above comments might be the one where the ratee is compared favorably to his peers.

Writing Bullets that Match the Rating

Depending on your unit and chain of command, a varying amount of emphasis is put on making NCOER bullet comments "match the rating". Since the ratings are Needs Improvement, Success, and Excellence, bullet comments are expected to be written so that they coincide with these ratings. The criteria for these ratings is shown in the table below:

Excellence	*Exceeds* Standards
Success	*Meets* Standards
Needs Improvement	*Doesn't Meet* Standards

To make a bullet comment match one of the above ratings, it has to agree, both in the level of achievement and/or in the language used to describe the achievement. Below are examples of bullet comments appropriate for each level of rating:

Excellence. Exceeds standards; demonstrated by specific example(s) and measurable results; achieved by only a few; clearly better than most. Examples:

- received Physical Fitness Badge
- qualified entire squad as expert with M-60
- awarded the expert Infantryman Badge (EIB)

Success. Meets all standards; fully competitive for schooling and promotion; counseling goal is to bring all NCOs to this level. Examples:

- shares experiences readily, constantly teaching soldiers
- constantly seeking to improve, completed three sub-courses during rating period
- coached and played on company softball team
- established a comprehensive cross training program for his section
- his platoon had only one vehicle on deadline report (for only 10 days) during last year

Needs Improvement. Missed meeting some standard. Examples:

- was unaware of whereabouts of subordinates on some occasions
- did not meet company deadline rate goals due to lack of focus
- did not achieve required fitness levels, lacked endurance/stamina

- unprepared to conduct formal training on three occasions

- failed to meet APFT standards for the two mile run and sit-ups with a total score of 148

As you can see, bullet comments for Excellence ratings must describe performance that is above and beyond what is normally expected. It must be an accomplishment that most people do not achieve. The bullets for a rating of success must demonstrate performance that, at least, meets standards.

Writing Bullets with Appropriate Language

In addition to describing performance that *earns* a particular rating as shown above, bullet comments must be written in language that is appropriate for the rating. Impact statements for Excellence bullets should use words like exceeded, surpassed, unparalleled, or best. These words or language that describes the highest level of performance indicate a rating of Excellence. If your bullet comment doesn't necessarily rate as Excellent, you can still adjust the language and use adjectives appropriate for an Excellent rating to suggest that it *is* an Excellent rating, thereby raising the level of your NCOER.

Below are examples, using our old bullet comment example, written in the language appropriate for each level of NCOER bullet comment, Excellence, Success, and Needs Improvement:

Excellence

A rating of Excellence is used for achievements that *exceeded* requirements and are represented by words such as exceeded, surpassed, bested, pinnacle of achievement, a record –any language that would indicate that the accomplishment *exceeded* normal requirements. Words like unmatched, unequaled, unrivaled, peerless also indicate superior performance.

"completed over 120 ops reports with 100% accuracy, *surpassed* unit goals, reduced unnecessary retransmissions by 50%"

"completed over 120 ops reports with 100% accuracy, streamlined procedures, reduced necessary man-hours and produced *best* rate in Battalion"

"completed over 120 ops reports with 100% accuracy, saved $10K in TDY costs by gathering info by teleconference, *a record* savings!"

"completed over 120 ops reports with 100% accuracy; maintained a 99% operational rate despite 50% manning deployed, an *unequaled* accomplishment"

"completed over 120 ops reports with 100% accuracy; *best* performer in section, directly responsible for unit's escalating success"

"completed over 120 ops reports with 100% accuracy; *best* on-time delivery rate in 5 years; a *peerless* performance!"

"completed over 120 ops reports with 100% accuracy, support was *unmatched* and key to success of OPERATION ANVIL TREE"

Note: These are not the only words that may be used to indicate superior, top performance. Use any words that describe the highest level of accomplishment. Other words or phrases might be *above average, dominant, exceptional,* etc.

Success

A rating of Success is used for accomplishments that *met* requirements and are represented by words such as, met, complied with, answered –anything that would indicate that the accomplishment *met* normal requirements. Words like maintained, ensured, continued, etc also indicate acceptable performance or performance that met standards.

"completed over 120 ops reports with 100% accuracy, solely responsible for section *meeting* transmission goals!" (meeting goals is the same as meeting standards and therefore describes a level of performance appropriate for a rating of Success.)

"completed over 120 ops reports with 100% accuracy, streamlined procedures, reduced necessary man-hours to *comply with* standards" ("comply with standards" means about the same as "meets standards" or "did what was required" and doesn't show an effort that goes beyond what is expected.)

"completed over 120 ops reports with 100% accuracy, saved $10K in TDY costs by gathering info by teleconference to *stay within budget*" ("stay within budget" is another way of saying "complying with limits" or "meets standards".)

"completed over 120 ops reports with 100% accuracy; *maintained* a 90% operational rate despite 50% manning deployed" ("maintained" is another way of saying "met standards" or "complied with requirements" or "continued as before", and indicates a status quo rather than any kind of improvement, much less exceeding standards.)

"completed over 120 ops reports with 100% accuracy; performance ensured platoon's continued success!" (lacks adjectives that stratifies performance such as best, superior, unmatched, etc. Also, the word "continued" implies a status quo and no improvement.)

"completed over 120 ops reports with 100% accuracy; motivation and teamwork ensured on-time delivery goals met 5 years straight" (the accomplishment is weakened by using the word "teamwork" to divide the credit among several people. In addition, the term "goals met" (rather than "goals exceeded") is appropriate for a Success bullet)

"completed over 120 ops reports with 100% accuracy, support key to success of OPERATION ANVIL TREE" (The term "support" does not specify individual achievement but suggests a team effort which weakens the bullet somewhat and makes it common enough to be a Success bullet comment.)

Needs Improvement

A rating of Needs Improvement is used for accomplishments that *do not meet* established requirements and is described by language like, did not complete all requirements, failed to meet goals, despite efforts could not perform at required level, etc –any language that indicates that the accomplishment *did not meet* requirements. Words like strived, has potential, progressed, improved, etc, are also used to indicate substandard performance.

"completed over 120 ops reports with 100% accuracy, maintained progress toward goal of 200 reports a year" ("maintained progress toward goal" indicates that the person being rated did not achieve the goal this rating period and needs improvement.)

"completed over 120 ops reports with 100% accuracy, with practice and further training, will reduce required completion time" ("with further practice and training" suggests that the person does not perform at the required level now and therefore needs improvement. The words, "will reduce" indicate that no improvement has been made yet but may be in the future. This further weakens the bullet.)

"completed over 120 ops reports with 100% accuracy, identified method that *may* reduce costs *if* implemented" (The words, "may" and "if" negate any statement that follows and weakens the bullet because they imply that no action actually occurred.)

"completed over 120 ops reports with 50% accuracy; maintained a 50% operational rate despite 50% manning deployed" (Describe an actual lack of achievement to demonstrate a need to improve.)

"completed over 120 ops reports with 100% accuracy; *has potential* to be a great operator" (Use the word, "potential", to indicate that a person *may* be a great operator some day but is not one now and therefore needs improvement.)

Appropriate Adjectives

On the following pages are lists of adjectives and adverbs that are appropriate for varying levels of performance. Note that these lists are only intended to demonstrate the graduations of descriptive words appropriate for escalating levels of performance and are not authoritative. In many cases, the words listed in the Success and Excellence columns can be used for either level of performance.

FREQUENCY		
Needs Improvement	**Success**	**Excellence**
seldom	often	always
sometimes	consistently	unfailingly
occasionally	regularly	constantly
never	frequently	continuously
rarely	usually	invariably
infrequently	commonly	habitually

MOTIVATION		
Needs Improvement	**Success**	**Excellence**
inadequate	energetic	aggressive
unconfident	confident	sure
uncooperative	cooperative	leading
combative	persuasive	driven
unsure	gung ho	forceful
undecided	purposeful	determined
unsatisfactory	satisfactory	enterprising
cautious	eager	enthusiastic
unmotivated	earnest	fearless
lazy	energized	insatiable
inactive	active	daring
unfocused	resilient	tenacious
uninterested	hard-charging	motivated
uninvolved	self-disciplined	potent
distracted	thriving	unlimited
unqualified	tireless	unstoppable
insufficient	sufficient	diligent
untrained	invested	committed

COMPARISON TO PEERS		
Needs Improvement	**Success**	**Excellence**
unequal	above average	unsurpassed
unnecessary	experienced	supreme
lagging	hard-charging	top/best
below average	hardy	unrivaled
sub par	heavyweight	dominant
inexperienced	excellent	premier/first
unmotivated	recognized	exceptional
team member	independent	incomparable
team player	indispensable	unmatched
potential	praiseworthy	leading
inactive	preeminent	matchless
active	invaluable	one-of-a-kind
uninspired	promising	out-performing
weak	proven	paramount
second class	seasoned	peerless
lightweight	skilled	unparalleled
slow	talented	prominent
undependable	strong	towering

PERFORMANCE		
Needs Improvement	**Success**	**Excellence**
ordinary	flawless	heroic
unsatisfactory	heavyweight	stellar
sub-par	proactive	industrious
lightweight	intent/driven	successful
imperfect	laudable	invaluable
unintentional	memorable	leading, top
inconsequential	methodical	innovative
unnoticed	meticulous	exceptional
poor	productive	masterful
forgettable	relentless	monumental
incomplete	professional	peerless
unproductive	notable	phenomenal
unprofessional	noteworthy	powerful
substandard	outstanding	prolific/tireless
unsuccessful	overpowering	triumphant
weak	praiseworthy	record-breaking
uninspired	quick/strong	remarkable
unenthusiastic	recognized	dynamic

CHARACTER		
Needs Improvement	**Success**	**Excellence**
dishonest	honest	idealistic
dishonorable	selfless	relentless
uncooperative	self-confident	impressive
careless	patient	purposeful
uninvolved	influential	outspoken
unconcerned	proactive	inspired
uninterested	interested	involved
immoral	invested	productive
immature	self-motivated	stable
inexperienced	level-headed	sincere
unproductive	logical	productive
negative	loyal	supportive
unmotivated	positive	motivated
unprofessional	perceptive	precise
selfish	efficient	trustworthy
counter-productive	self-reliant	serious
unreliable	optimistic	persuasive
undependable	realistic	reliable
emotional	reasonable	resilient

COMPETENCE		
Needs Improvement	**Success**	**Excellence**
uncooperative	able	above average
inattentive	competent	advanced
uninvolved	capable	authoritative
slow	accomplished	battle-tested
incapable	adaptable	versatile
unqualified	adept	exceptional
unproductive	alert	prepared
untrained	analytical	effective
unprofessional	bright	brilliant
ineffective	dynamic	essential
erratic	educated	proven
inaccurate	efficient	goal-oriented
incompetent	experienced	expert
inefficient	organized	masterful
unskilled	imaginative	innovative
unprepared	informed	proficient
inexperienced	intelligent	knowledgeable
disorganized	inventive	productive
uninformed	learned	multi-talented

PHYSICAL FITNESS & MILITARY BEARING		
Needs Improvement	**Success**	**Excellence**
uninspired	intense	ambitious
weak	bulletproof	daring
discourteous	courteous	model
disrespectful	respectful	example
unprepared	dutiful	improved
negative	indefatigable	relentless
substandard	poised	tactful
counter-productive	polished	tenacious
unmotivated	energetic	aggressive
failing	resilient	talented
disorderly	diligent	soldierly
antisocial	tireless	warrior
insubordinate	tough	tested
undisciplined	disciplined	veteran
unprofessional	professional	well-qualified
complaining	articulate	eloquent
unenthusiastic	cooperative	spokesman
combative	prepared	ready
immature	strong	determined

LEADERSHIP		
Needs Improvement	**Success**	**Excellence**
immature	articulate	eloquent
untrustworthy	assured	efficient
unobservant	dedicated	committed
uncommitted	loyal	confident
selfish	compassionate	courageous
unconfident	competent	daring
dependant	cooperative	decisive
abusive	deliberate	determined
unqualified	diplomatic	discreet
unsuccessful	enabling	dominant
combative	encouraging	bold
uncooperative	facilitating	successful
irresponsible	effective	generous
uncaring	firm	independent
incompetent	impartial	influential
unyielding	fair	powerful
indecisive	judicious	trustworthy
inconsistent	considerate	responsible
unjust	prudent	recognized

TRAINING		
Needs Improvement	**Success**	**Excellence**
inconsistent	consistent	diligent
distracted	focused	driven
incomplete	complete	ready
haphazardly	meticulous	certified
unaccomplished	accomplished	qualified
inaccurate	accurate	fluent
unobservant	observant	detail-oriented
irresponsible	responsible	seasoned
failed	continuous	proven/tested
non-progressive	progressive	flexible
stagnant	proactive	prolific
unqualified	trained	advanced
neglected	attentive	aggressive
untrained	error-free	dedicated
unmotivated	overcame	inspired
decertified	complies	interested
unsuccessful	successful	promising
indifferent	enthusiastic	relentless
impatient	patient	thorough

RESPONSIBILITY		
Needs Improvement	**Success**	**Excellence**
unprofessional	firm	commendable
inconsistent	conscientious	responsible
wasteful	conservative	dependable
deceptive	observant	key
unfair	impartial	committed
inexperienced	accountable	courageous
inattentive	careful	diligent
unobservant	cooperative	consistent
irresponsible	attentive	dedicated
unethical	diplomatic	essential
immoral	earnest	productive
careless	efficient	effective
reckless	experienced	invested
undependable	mature	reliable
unreliable	proactive	alert
untrustworthy	professional	resourceful
unaccountable	protective	trustworthy
inconsiderate	supportive	practical
immature	punctual	vigilant

Duty Descriptions

The first real writing done in the NCOER is the duty description. The duty description must describe your most important duties or the NCOER will lack impact from the very start. This block is the only place where we're allowed to list what we do so make it count. Yes, accomplishments will be listed in the body of the NCOER which somewhat describe what we do but it won't provide the whole picture. In the Bullet Comments blocks, we only describe the highlights. Fit in as much as you can beginning with the most important information. If you supervise troops or perform any supervisory oversight, make sure you include that information.

Filling in Part III

This information is written by the rater and verified with the rated Soldier. Refer to DA PAM 623-3, Evaluation Reporting System, table 3–3 for duty description evaluation instructions. The duty description:

- Is an outline of the normal requirements of the specific duty position.

- Should show type of work required rather than frequently changing tasks.

- Is essential to performance counseling and evaluation. It is used during the first counseling session to tell the rated NCO what the duties are and what needs to be emphasized.

- May be updated during the rating period.

- Is used at the end of the rating period to record what was important about the duties.

NCOER Part : IIIc: Daily Duties and Scope

These must include a series of phrases, starting with verbs/action words and separated by semicolons and ending in a period. This block should address the most important routine duties and responsibilities. Ideally, this should include the number of people supervised, equipment, facilities, and dollars involved and any other routine duties and responsibilities.

Readiness NCO or training NCO. For ARNGUS AGR Soldiers assigned as readiness NCO or training NCO, enter both the NCO's TOE or TDA assignment and the full-time support titles such as Chief or Firing Battery/Readiness NCO. Include a mix of both the position duties and the full-time support duties in Part IIIc, d, and e.

NCOER Part : IIId: Areas of Special Emphasis

Enter areas of special emphasis/appointed duties. These must include a list of tasks/duties separated by semicolons and ending with a period. This block is the most likely to change during the rating period. It should include the most important items that applied at any time during the rating period. ARNGUS AGR Soldiers assigned as readiness NCO or training NCO, enter both the NCO's TOE or TDA assignment and the full-time support titles such as Chief or Firing Battery/Readiness NCO. Include a mix of both the position duties and the full-time support duties in Part IIIc, d, and e.

NCOER Part : IIIe: Appointed Duties

Include duties appointed that are not normally included in the duty description. For ARNGUS AGR Soldiers assigned as Readiness NCO or Training NCO, enter both the NCO's TOE or TDA assignment and the full-time support titles such as Chief or Firing Battery/Readiness NCO. Include a mix of both the position duties and the full-time support duties in Part III, d, and e.

NCOER Part : IIIf: Counseling Dates

Enter the actual dates of the counseling obtained from the DA Form 2166-8-1 (YYYYMMDD). When counseling dates are omitted, the senior rater will enter a statement in part Ve, explaining why counseling was not accomplished. The absence of counseling will not be used as the sole basis for an appeal. However, the lack of counseling may be used to help support other claims made in an appeal.

Remember: be specific and if you participated in OIF/OEF at a deployed location, make sure it's stated in the duty description. Make sure the duty MOS is correct.

Duty Description Examples

Because duty descriptions are unique to a particular MOS or duty position, it's not possible to include examples for all in this book. Below are examples of some of the most common duty descriptions in order to give the reader an idea of what is commonly included in duty descriptions.

MOS 42A Human Resources Specialist

Serves as a Human Resources Sergeant for the Personnel Administration Center in the Combat Aviation Brigade Rear Detachment; *provides* support to 200 Soldiers and Officers; *performs* duties of and supervises personnel support activity; *maintains* enlisted rating scheme; *provides* daily readiness reports (PERSTAT) to G1, to include monthly Personnel Management Indicator (PMI) reports; *reviews* award and promotion correspondence, exceptions to policy, personnel actions, consolidated reports, QNSR and finance issues; responsible for the training and welfare of one NCO and four Soldiers.

MOS 92Y Unit Supply Specialist

Serves as Supply Sergeant in a Forward Support Company in support of the 155th Combat Aviation Brigade of the 101st Airborne Division (AASLT); *manages* over $5 million worth of organizational and installation property; *monitors* and administers a $10,000 IMPAC Card Budget within the battalion; requests, *receives and processes* equipment for issue and turn-in; *assists* in conducting request and delivery of all classes of supply; responsible for the supervision, training, morale and welfare of five Soldiers; responsible for the accountability of two five ton vehicles, one HMWVV, a trailer, one 10K generator and various office automation equipment valued in excess of $500,000.

Responsible for over $2M worth of critical unit property and the supervision of 24 personnel; ensures all readiness requirements are planned for; directs subordinates in performance of assigned functions; coordinates preparation of unit movement plans, load plans, and Automated Unit Equipment List reports; evaluates the efficiency of unit supply activities; provides input for Unit Status Report (USR), monitors the Army Maintenance System for all unit equipment, schedules and ensures preventive maintenance on all weapons systems; ensures subordinate personnel receive training necessary for professional development.

MOS 63B Light Wheel Vehicle Mechanic

Performs duties as the Battalion Motor Sergeant for the Special Operations Battalion consolidated Motor Pool; responsible for the health, welfare, professional development, training, and morale of five NCOs and five Soldiers; ensures the planning, coordination, and management of scheduled and unscheduled organizational maintenance for six pacing items and over 500 pieces of reportable equipment; manages The Army Maintenance Management System (TAMMS), and Shop Stock Listing (SSL); responsible for the mission readiness of government property valued in excess of $155,000.

MOS68W Health Care Specialist

Responsible for the training, health, and welfare of a five Soldier medic section in a FORSCOM combat support (CORPS) Military Police company subject to worldwide contingency deployments; administers emergency and routine medical treatment to battle and non-battle casualties; assists with outpatient care and treatment; supervises the control of medication and Class VIII medical supplies valued at over $50,000; responsible for the training and certifying of Soldiers in Advanced Combat Lifesaver techniques.

Responsible for the health, welfare, and morale of four platoon level medics in a light infantry company; responsible for the medical readiness and welfare of a light infantry company; ensures that individual medical equipment valued in excess of $50,000 are accounted for and maintained to unit standards; responsible for the tactical training and physical fitness of his medics; counsels and guides four soldiers in professional development.

MOS 92G Food Service Operations

Assigned as a Food Service Sergeant for the 5th Brigade Dining Facility; responsible for supervising 10 personnel in a consolidated dining facility; serves 10 separate units feeding approximately 2500 Soldiers daily. Serves as a team leader as part of a maneuver platoon that directly supports 2-14 FA; performs duty as a senior gunner for maneuver platoon, responsible for the health, welfare, counseling, and development of four Soldiers; enforces all Army standards and assists the section sergeant in all squad matters.

Performs duties as the Food Operations Sergeant for a Heavy Equipment Transport (HET) Company; responsible for the supervision, training, and welfare of one NCO and three Soldiers; accountable for field feeding equipment valued in excess of $250,000; establishes operating and work procedures, inspects dining, storage areas, and dining facility personnel; determines subsistence requirements; requests, receives, and accounts for subsistence items; prepares, cooks, and serves food in a field or garrison environment; provides technical guidance to subordinates in garrison and field kitchen operations.

MOS92A Automated Logistical Specialist

Serves as the Materiel Management Supervisor in a Multi-Class II, IV, and IX Supply Support Activity for Bravo Company, 503d Brigade Support Battalion; responsible for the health, morale, and welfare of three NCOs and five Soldiers; assists the accountable officer in managing 2,500 Authorized Stockage Lines (ASL) valued at $15 million; accountable for two Standard Army Management Information systems (STAMIS), five 10k forklifts, and two M129A4 vans valued at $1.5 million.

Operations Sergeant

Serves as the Operations Sergeant of a deployed Corps Support Battalion with an assigned strength of over 1,500 Soldiers in support of Operation Iraqi Freedom V; provides technical and doctrinal advice to the S3 and commander; assists the Battle Captain with rehearsals and execution of actual battle drills; responsible for the supervision of 5 NCOs and 1 enlisted Soldier; assists and supervises the Plans NCOs in the MDMP; prepares the TOC for orders, drills, briefs, and rehearsals; receives and appropriately handles and distributes FRAGOs, Red Cross messages and Serious Incident Reports (SIRs); supervises and ensures the Commanders Update Briefing (CUB) is rehearsed and allocates time to brief the commander(s) and staff.

Serves as Operations Sergeant in a deployed Combat Sustainment Support Battalion, comprised of ten companies and an assigned strength of 1,500 Soldiers in support of Operation Iraqi Freedom VI; principal enlisted advisor to the Battle Captain; coordinates battle space assets and tracks movements of Combat Logistic Patrols (CLPs); collects and reports line of sight communications data used for optimizing real-world FM networks; ensures timely reporting of sensitive items, serious incidents, and training statistics; responsible for the health and welfare, training and operational readiness of six NCOs and one Soldier; performs duties as the Battle Captain in his absence.

Readiness NCO

Serves as the Readiness NCO of a Combat Sustainment Support Battalion with an assigned strength of over 1,500 Soldiers; advises the commander on training, logistics, personnel, and mobilization readiness requirements; reviews and implements mobilization directives and regulations; obtains necessary data for the unit status report and assists the commander in preparing readiness reports as required; drafts training schedules to comply with command and higher headquarters guidance; maintains the unit training library and related training equipment and aids; tests, operates, maintains, and deploys JISCC.

Motor Sergeant

Serves as a Motor Sergeant for a forward-deployed, tactical signal company; provides tactical contingency C2 communications to the United States Army Europe (USAREUR) within the EUCOM and CENTCOM area of responsibility; responsible for the scheduled and unscheduled maintenance of 55 M113 Armored Personnel Carriers, 55 pieces of rolling stock, ground support and material handling equipment, and equipment valued at $5,000,000; responsible for service, deadline and USR reports as well as overall motor pool effectiveness; responsible for the training, welfare, discipline, combat readiness and development of 15 Soldiers.

Platoon Sergeant

Responsible for the morale, health, and training of a 30 man Rifle Platoon; responsible for the maintenance, accountability, and effective utilization of all platoon-assigned weapons, night observation devices, communications equipment, and individual equipment worth over $500,000; counsels, disciplines, and develops soldiers and NCOs into competent leaders; maintains the highest state of combat readiness regardless of conditions and personnel changes.

Drill Sergeant

Performs duties as a Drill Sergeant in a Basic Combat Training Company; trains over 60 Initial Entry Soldiers in a 10-week cycle; supervises and instructs Initial Entry Soldiers in all subjects required to complete Basic Combat Training; develops recruits in discipline, physical fitness, military bearing, personal hygiene, first aid, pride in military and country; trains recruits in drill and ceremonies, basic rifle marksmanship and maintenance of assigned equipment; provides instruction on military history, customs, courtesies and military regulations; accountable for $150,000 of equipment.

Rear Detachment Sergeant Major

Serves as the Rear Detachment Sergeant Major for a 550 man Combined Arms Battalion during a twelve month deployment to Iraq; responsible for the supervision, accountability, health, and welfare of 5 Non Commissioned Officer Cadre members and up to 100 rear detachment Soldiers with the primary mission of preparing and training Soldiers for deployment, separating Soldiers from the Army through the Chapter Process, and assisting Wounded Veterans to heal and return to their assigned units while simultaneously supporting family members of deployed Soldiers in a range of personal issues to include Casualty Assistance and Notifications.

Recruiter

Recruits, determines applicant enlistment eligibility, counsels applicants on enlistment programs and options, prepares enlistment applications and processes qualified applicants to enlist in the Army and Army Reserve; accounts for and prepares Future Soldiers for initial entry training; implements and conducts Army awareness programs throughout an area covering 55 square miles with a population of 55,000; maintains a network of influencers to include parents, educators, and community officials in three high schools and one college; responsible for $50,000 worth of government equipment.

Training NCO

Develops and maintains all training records; monitors, schedules, and prepares training; assists Soldiers in personnel actions and schedules service school attendance; advises the Operations Readiness NCO on deployment training requirements and readiness; plans and executes unit mobilization plans; attends schools and conferences as required; operates ATRRS and other training systems; maintains positive control of over $50,000 worth of equipment.

First Sergeant

First Sergeant of a Forward Deployed Headquarters and Headquarters Company in a Special Troops Battalion tasked with providing support to an HBCT; responsible for the discipline, training, mentoring, personal and professional development, health, welfare, and morale of 150 Soldiers; sets and enforces high standards on conduct, training, professional development and operations; controls and synchronizes facilities, equipment, and vehicles valued in excess of $500,000; assists the commander in planning, coordinating, and supervising all activities that support the unit's mission.

Values

Values describe character. Values are qualities such as loyalty, integrity, courage, and motivation. Army values are the foundation of America's Army, the solid rock upon which everything else stands. Values are the glue that binds us together as members of a noble profession. They make the whole much greater than the sum of the parts. They are nonnegotiable; they apply to everyone, all the time, and in every situation.

o a classic example of a true NCO representing the top 20% of NCOs in the brigade

o a loyal and committed NCO

o a man of true integrity, living the morals and values he teaches to others

o a real team player; makes positive contributions

o a team player who shows great pride in the unit

o absolute dedication and loyalty to the chain of command, unit, and mission

o absolutely dedicated to the mission and unit success

o accepts all challenges and responsibilities without hesitation

o aggressively seeks out new and difficult challenges and responsibilities

o always gives 100% to ensure mission accomplishment

o always maintains very high standards of personal conduct on and off duty o always open and candid when asked questions or expressing his opinions

o always places unit mission and Soldier welfare first

o answered the call to duty without hesitation in support of the Deepwater Horizon Oil Spill

o attains results regardless of the mission or tasks

o can be depended upon to perform under the most extreme circumstances

o can be relied on to successfully complete all assignments

o committed NCO that lives by "Mission first, Soldiers always"

o committed to excellence and exudes quality in all actions and assigned tasks

o committed to excellence and mission accomplishment

o committed to mission accomplishment

o committed to the Army and the mission

o committed to the unit's mission

o committed to training and caring for Soldiers and their families

o conducts himself as a well groomed senior NCO

o consistently displayed a sense of loyalty seldom seen in others of his rank and station

o consistently makes things happen with positive results

o consistently sets the example by leading from the front and doing the right thing

o constantly demonstrates a professional attitude; asset to any unit o continually demonstrates leadership and integrity beyond reproach

o continually exhibits the highest standards of loyalty, integrity and personal behavior

o continuously seeks out new and difficult challenges and responsibilities

o dedicated professional with high moral standards

o dedicated team player who fosters esprit de corps

o dedicated to mission accomplishment

o dedicated to team concept

o dedicated to the values and traditions of the Army

o dedicated to this unit and its mission

o delayed college enrollment to cover manning deficiency

o demonstrated extreme loyalty to team and unit

o displays initiative and takes responsibility for his actions

o displayed a high degree of professionalism and demanded the same of others

o displayed an outstanding devotion to duty

o displayed extreme professionalism in every aspect during the rated period

o displayed the utmost devotion to the mission and the Soldiers

o displays a high degree of honesty, loyalty, and integrity

o displays exceptional pride in his Soldiers, his job, and the Army

o displays sincerity in ambitions and objectives

o driven to succeed by self-motivation and strong sense of purpose

o dynamic character and stamina in overcoming any challenge

o effectively executed all goals or missions assigned, regardless of difficulty

o embodies the highest standards of loyalty, integrity, and personal behavior

o enforces strict adherence to Army regulations

o enjoys challenges no matter how difficult

o exceptionally reliable and trustworthy when given an assignment

o executed all tasks with vigor and integrity

o exercised mature judgment and meticulous attention to detail

o exhibits a high level of esprit de corps which carries over to his section

o exhibits high standards of behavior; a model Soldier and extraordinary leader

o exhibits highest standard of loyalty to superiors and the organization

o exhibits moral courage, stands up for what is right

o exhibits the skill, temperament, and reliability of a true professional

o extremely honest and trustworthy

o extremely loyal to unit

o extremely reliable and industrious, performs extremely well under pressure o focused on mission accomplishment, consistently achieving superior results

o focuses on mission accomplishment with superior results

o fully supported the Army's Equal Opportunity program in word and deed

o furthered his education during his off-duty time in order to enhance team

o goes the extra mile to complete the job

o handles situations firmly and fair; unequaled in promoting harmony and teamwork

o has an unwavering devotion to his job and his responsibilities to his team members

o has the courage to stand up for his Soldiers and himself

o has the courage to voice his opinions and the patience to present his views logically

o has the moral courage to state his opinions honestly and freely

o has unquestionable loyalty to her unit and the Army

o has unquestioning faith in her chain of command and Army values

o her personal integrity is unquestionable

o highest of standards and conduct on and off duty

o highly dedicated and professional NCO

o highly motivated and honest

o highly motivated Noncommissioned Officer

o highly task/mission focused

o his conduct, on and off duty, is above reproach

o innovative and determined in pursuit of Army goals

o insists on loyalty to supervisors and peers

o instilled a sense of pride within his section

o instills spirit of teamwork in his Soldiers

o integrity is above reproach

o integrity is unquestionable

o is a member of the team and shows pride in unit

o is a Soldier first, proud to serve, resolute in his duty

o is both competent and dependable

o is the best Operations NCO I have ever encountered

o leads from the front, accomplishes all mission tasks

o loyal to supervisors and peers

o loyal to the unit and the ideals of the NCO Corps

o loyal to the unit and the NCO Corps

o loyal, dedicated, and dependable NCO

o loyal, honest, and sincere NCO

o loyal, truthful, and fair

o maintains a fierce and steadfast belief in assigned mission

o maintains highest standards

o meets challenges without compromising integrity

o mission accomplishment is a direct result of his dedication to duty

o motivates and challenges subordinates through leadership by example

o never hesitates to voice an honest opinion

o not afraid to confront sensitive issues; understands the importance of truth and accuracy

o on short notice, reacted and put together an Honor Guard for the funeral of a military retiree

o offers advice, but loyal to final decisions made by superiors

o often works late to ensure his Soldiers' professional and personal needs are met

o outstanding problem solver; dynamic planner and organizer

o performance above the normal call of duty produced exemplary achievements

o personal conduct is above reproach

o personal conduct on and off duty, reflects favorably on the NCO Corps

o personal lifestyle epitomizes the total NCO

o places Army, mission, and subordinates above personal interest

o places unit's mission, welfare, and training of his Soldiers above personal needs

o positive attitude toward mission accomplishment

o possessed unselfish dedication to duty and quality maintenance

o possesses absolute dedication and loyalty to the unit, the mission, and the Soldiers

o possesses pride in service and a sense of duty that inspires his peers

o possesses strong moral principles and personal values

o possesses the moral courage to always do what is right

o possesses unselfish dedication and loyalty to the unit and the mission

o practices equal opportunity throughout the platoon

o practices fair and just treatment to all Soldiers

o preserves momentum when those around him falter

o proactive in performing duties prior to becoming a directive

o professional conduct above reproach

o professional Soldier 24 hours a day

o puts the Army first

o puts the Army, mission, and Soldiers before own personal interests

o reenlisted to stay with her unit until mission was finished

o rejected transfer to rear to remain behind with his team

o remained flexible and cooperative under any circumstance

o respected for his candor and integrity

o risked life so that others may live on countless occasions

o risked personal safety to ensure safety of visiting unit and their mission

o seeks challenges no matter the difficulty

o self-motivated; willing to go the distance

o selflessly committed to training and caring for Soldiers and their families

o sets superb example for subordinates

o sets the example for taking initiative and accepting responsibility o shows genuine concern for subordinates

o sincere, truthful, and fair

o stands behind principles; outwardly determined and loyal

o stands firmly on his convictions

o stands for what is right

o stands up for his personal convictions

o staunch believer in team building within his platoon

o strives for team effort in accomplishing assigned tasks

o strong in character, pride and professionalism

o strong supporter of Equal Opportunity

o strongly supports the Army Equal Employment Opportunity program

o superior performance of duty

o supports and encourages allegiance to mission

o takes great pride in supporting Soldiers

o takes the initiative and makes things happen

o the epitome of what every NCO should be; aggressive, intelligent, and professional

o totally committed to team effort

o totally dedicated to the Army

o totally dedicated to unit, mission and Soldiers; a credit to the NCO Corps

o totally professional and demands the same of his Soldiers

o totally professional on and off duty

o trusted by his superiors to lead platoon and make the right decisions o uncompromising passion to mission accomplishment

o unequaled loyalty; dedicated and caring leader

o unfailing loyalty to the chain of command, its goals, and Soldiers

o unquestionable loyalty

o unquestioned integrity and exemplary personal conduct both on and off duty

o unselfishly devoted an extraordinary amount of time to increasing the functionality of the unit area

o utmost competence in his duties even under the most extreme circumstances

o utterly dependable under all circumstances

o valued for her commitment and loyalty

o volunteered for difficult civic project to improve Army's image abroad

o willing to sacrifice time and effort to attain unit goals

o willing to spend additional effort and time to accomplish all assigned tasks

o works efficiently and effectively with superiors and is selflessly committed to the unit's mission

o works harmoniously and effectively with others

o works long hours ensuring Soldiers are taken care of

o works until the job is accomplished

o works until the mission is completed

Needs Improvement (Values)

o has good potential but requires more experience applying daily Soldier leadership skills

o good Soldier, but fails to improve by applying sound personal management skills

o demonstrated a serious lack of integrity and poor judgment without consideration of results

o compromised integrity by submitting altered documents; poor example to subordinates

o encouraged Soldiers to advance by cheating for each other, poor example

o hid serious shortfalls until it was too late to correct them

o avoids complying with orders, regularly shows disrespect to NCOs, requires constant supervision

o is a motivated troop but needs further guidance in...

o an excellent technician but needs to work on tact and communication skills

o has unlimited potential but requires more experience before...

o must realize the importance of finishing assigned tasks without supervision

o failed to use time wisely, consistently failed to complete duty assignments

o frequent unwillingness to cooperate in working toward unit goals affected readiness

Competence

Competence is the ability to perform in the current duty assignment and in other assignments within the MOS when required. Competence includes skills such as reading, writing, speaking, and basic math. Competence involves not only knowledge but also doing the job correctly and completely to the best of one's ability. It also includes sound judgment and the ability to weigh alternatives and make good decisions. Closely associated with competence is the desire to learn more and approach tasks with innovative ideas. Examples of bullet comments associated with competence follow:

o 100% first time go on FY09 command inspection; acting supply sergeant on numerous occasions with outstanding results

o absolute quality performance in all MOS tasks

o accepted all obstacles as challenges; accepts nothing less than total success

o accomplished 125 of 150 upgrade/qualification tasks; 75% completed on three airframes; ahead of peers

o accomplished all tasks assigned with total accuracy

o achieved 100% SIDPERS suspense for 12 consecutive months; awarded Army Achievement Medal

o achieved an outstanding rating on 3 out of 4 command inspections, best in the battalion

o achieved commendable rating as unit security manager on Battalion Command Inspection Program

o achieved Senior Instructor level at the USAOCS ahead of peers o achieved superior results when confronted with major responsibilities and limited resources

o achieved three honor platoon awards during rating period

o achieves exceptional results toward mission accomplishment 100% of the time

o advanced through duty positions as Survey Team Member, Survey Team Chief, and finally, Operations NCO during his assignment

o advised a multi-agency foreign intelligence exploitation team, received national intel community accolades

o aided the 55th Sustainment Brigade by establishing a functional helpdesk which supported over 3000 soldiers

o alerted, assembled, and deployed the company to support Operation Just Endeavor during the Commander's absence

o all his areas inspected during last battalion command inspection were rated best in battalion

o always displayed a high degree of technical knowledge of maintenance

o always displayed high level of initiative

o always in focus and is superbly well organized; never without direction

o always prepared to accept any task given

o always strives for self-improvement

o amplified local medical capability by assisting with the care of 200 trauma and outpatient local nationals and coalition forces

o analyzed and identified enemy point-of-origin sites, assisted in elimination of enemy attack zones and support, reduced IDF attacks by 50%

o as acting First Sergeant, corrected numerous problems and laid a good foundation for the new 1SG

o as acting First Sergeant, demonstrated rare competence by leading the unit through turbulent times

o assisted in medical evacuation of over 100 U.S. and Multi-National Coalition Soldiers from MNC-I Forward Operating Bases

o assisted Tobyhanna Army Depot maintenance team; replaced azimuth motor electric brake assembly; solved satellite autotrack failure

o attention to detail and immediate response to pay and personnel issues provided a sense of security and improved morale throughout the Company

o authored the new Patch Barracks Community Physical Security Plan

o awarded AAM by DC for outstanding administration of unit's NCO-ER program

o awarded Bronze Badge of Excellence in CG's marksmanship competition

o awarded the Bronze Star Medal for actions during Operation IRAQI FREEDOM III

o awarded TRADOC Certificate of Achievement for First Quarter 04 reenlistments

o battalion recognized by CSA as Army's best electronic warfare unit

o battery named best at ground defense by the Commanding General at Ft Sill

o certified over 75 items of TMDE, key to laboratory's 3 day backlog; lowest backlog in 5 years o chosen as a brigade 2006 DLI Language Olympics team member due to his language skills

o chosen as Observer Controller to assist a FSB which resulted in a successful JRTC rotation

o cleared over 2000 miles during route clearance missions during three months of combat operations resulting in the safe discovery of two IED's and zero casualties

o commended by Battalion Commander for his platoon's flawless execution of STX lane training

o commended by Battalion CSM for excellent performance as acting First Sergeant

o commended by the Battalion Commander for his Leaderbook; now used as an example for others to follow

o commended for developing a Suicide Prevention Program that was adopted throughout the command

o committed to excellence; anything less is unacceptable

o communicated with all units within the AOR; provided situational awareness of airspace control, attack aviation status, and ongoing operations during JRTC 10-08

o competence and motivation unequaled; stands out among his peers

o completed 18 semester hours of college towards an associate degree maintaining a 3.5 grade point average despite a demanding work schedule and TDY

o completed the Electronic Key Distribution Course helping to automate COMSEC Key distribution throughout the Afghanistan Theater of Operations

o completed over 50 combat missions while assigned to an Infantry Company in the Sunni Triangle during OIF 03-06

o completed over 500 assignments as section NCOIC

o completed requirements for Associates Degree

o completed Signal Leadership Course, Special Forces Operations Course by correspondence during this period

o completed the 100 mile, joint unit Nijmegen March with the first group of finishers

o completed all tasks on time and beyond expectations

o composed the draft and final version of the Medical Tactical Standard Operating Procedure used by all units deployed under the HHC 844th Engineer Battalion

o conducted 15 sniper missions to limit terrorist movement in Company AO; decreased IED activity by 50%

o conducted an air insertion mission and cleared an entire village to prevent insurgents from conducting future operations in the Battalion AO

o conducted over 50 aeromedical evacuation missions achieving maximum results while flying over 250 combat hours

o conducted traffic control for over twenty major command ceremonies with no traffic incidents

o considered to be the best First Sergeant by all outside organizations we support

o consistently displayed sound, mature judgment

o consistently enrolled in MOS, military, and civilian courses

o constantly seeks self-improvement; always willing to grow, learn, and improve

o continually demonstrates competence and knowledge of First Sergeant duties

o continuously sought out by peers and superiors throughout the Battalion for operational guidance o coordinated the safe movement of over 5,000 passengers with the Deployment Center and Base Ops

o created the unit NCO Battle Book which was adopted by the entire 614th Field Artillery

o crime prevention program rated best on the installation by the Provost Marshall's Office

o currently maintaining an "A" average in college

o delegated effectively; developed his subordinates to lead

o delivered over 2M gallons of JP-8 aviation fuel to 10K aircraft annually; maintained impressive 15-minute average response time

o demonstrated excellent technical and tactical knowledge as a squad leader ensuring all tasks were completed in a timely manner and exceeding all standards

o demonstrated sound judgment and growth

o demonstrated exemplary leadership and competency while activated for annual training

o demonstrates outstanding aptitude for operational and administrative work

o designed, contracted, and installed computer systems for 2 APODs and ASP Headquarters

o despite not being a supply sergeant, helped supply the 163rd Rear Detachment with supplies needed for new Soldiers and daily operations

o developed 11B/13B BNCOC FTX-STX that became the model for all Noncommissioned Officer Academies

o developed a database program for security that was implemented as brigade standard o developed a unique and efficient approach to debriefing crewmembers returning from missions involving injuries or fatalities

o developed an automated review of 5 databases, reviewed over 20,000 QM positions Army wide

o developed and organized operational support for over 20 FTXs

o developed and published mission SOP for use by Watch NCOs of Echelon-Above-Corps intelligence unit

o developed the first-ever maintenance SOP, created a standardized system for the Iraqi Border Patrol

o developed training management system which led unit to excellence rating during CI

o developed two theater-level order of battle databases; improved deployment success

o dexterity and competence led to his selection as a Flight Instructor over 5 of his peers for the unit's Aircrew Training Program

o did not waiver from responsibility for himself; learned from his mistakes and sought self-improvement

o directed the conversion of Microsoft Office 2003 to 2007 on over 100 computers; ensured file integrity and minimal downtime for the Battalion end users

o directly responsible for the unit's extremely successful deployment to NTC

o displayed high training skills and technical knowledge

o displayed outstanding organizational abilities; ensured the maintenance and upkeep of 15 wheeled vehicles and trailers with a property book value of $1,500,000 o displayed the ability to perform at a level of greater responsibility in the absence of his supervisor

o displayed the highest levels of professional competence in execution of his duties

o displays tactical and technical knowledge well beyond his skill level

o distinguished honor graduate of his BNCOC course

o distinguished Honor Graduate of the Traffic Management Accident Investigation Course

o Drill Sergeant of the Quarter, Southeast Region Command

o during the Fort Gordon Signal Symposium his section received laudatory comments from the Commanding General

o eagerly accomplished all assigned tasks

o earned a Commendable rating for TRANSEC key control during Battalion Command Inspection Program

o earned a rating of "exceeds the standard" on three additional duty areas during command inspections

o earned an Air Medal for his exemplary performance in combat and dedication to duty during Operation Iraqi Freedom

o earned commendable ratings on all HAZMAT and Safety inspections

o earned Honor Graduate at the Foreign Language Training Center, Europe

o earned M60 MG Master which placed him in the top 10% of the Division's NCOs

o earned Recruiter Gold Badge at Colorado Springs post in less than 12 months o earned runner up for 1st Armored Division NCO of the Year award

o efficient time management enabled him to complete 12 credit hours toward a BS degree in Medical Technology with a 3.5 GPA

o endured long hours of work dedicated to accomplish the unit's mission of law and order operations during Annual Training 2010

o enhanced the combat readiness and support of deployed Soldiers and soldier systems supporting operations in Iraq and Afghanistan

o ensured a rapid and professional deployment of individual teams to the area of operations during OIF II

o ensured the team was prepared for all missions and contingencies prior to movement; ensured mission success

o established a MOS training program within the squad decreasing the NMC vehicles by 50% and increasing the technical knowledge of subordinates

o established company and battalion level battle drills in response to evolving enemy TTPs

o exceeded course standards with academic average of 98% at Battle Staff NCO School

o exceeding the standard in technical and tactical knowledge of his 240B machine gun

o excelled as First Sergeant when company 1SG was absent

o excelled while acting independently and without specific instructions

o excels in the absence of orders and guidance

o expert performance resulted in first place victory in USAISC worldwide supply excellence competition o expertise and dedication were factors in success of two week DA-level NBC test

o expertly bore sighted systems; accuracy made live-target firing unnecessary, saved over $20K in ammo

o extraordinary initiative; competent and proficient in all duties

o extremely competent and dedicated NCO

o extremely competent; performed all duties above expected standards and expectations

o facilitated prescreening of 200 military members; key to the success of six whole blood drives, two of which occurred during indirect fire

o facilitated the flow of Soldiers in and out of theater

o first unit NCO to earn I Corps Distinguished Leader by demonstrating effective leadership skills

o flawlessly handled finance and personnel actions for 250 soldiers with zero late transactions

o General Smith highly commended his TOC operation during the recent I Corps BCTP exercise

o handled extremely stressful, potentially dangerous situations during Operation ANACONDA with ease

o has an extensive knowledgebase from previous deployments and does not hesitate to share lessons learned

o has outstanding organizational skills; maximizes limited resources to create excellent results

o helped establish a unit notification program which was adopted by the TRADOC PERMAS Team

o her consistent performance has been invaluable to daily operations of the company o her knowledge of Squad Leader duties/skills is sought by subordinates and peers alike

o highest score ever achieved in Drill Competition in his first 4 weeks as Drill Sergeant

o highly skilled in all tasks required of a Senior Instructor

o highly skilled in planning, arranging required equipment and personnel and conducting aircraft maintenance

o his astute attention to detail and management resulted in his crew maintaining 100% operational readiness rate during Operation Diesel

o his attention to detail and invaluable experience played a vital role in the successful deployment of his team for OIF

o his competence enabled him to rank 3rd of 20 recruiters in mission accomplishment

o his dedication led to the successful redeployment of the battalion back to Ft Stewart

o his intelligence reports were cited by Pentagon analysts as the most relevant in 5 years

o his invaluable experience and technical knowledge led to his selection and certification as unit CPR instructor

o his knowledge and efforts to improve himself and the NCO Corps were key in his being recommended for promotion to Staff Sergeant

o his knowledge and tactical expertise while attached to an Infantry Company has equated to success in over 30 combat missions

o his organizational skills and attention to detail enhanced overall unit effectiveness

o his position assigned to officers in other battalions

o his professionalism and duty performance in combat during Operation Northern Watch earned him an Air Medal

o his sound judgment and tactical savvy kept his crew alive during 10 IED attacks and his keen eye identified another 5 IEDs before detonation

o his tactical and technical expertise led to his selection as an Observer/Controller for an NTC rotation of the 55th Med Co (AA)

o his tactical proficiency was continually sought after by subordinates and superiors; continually incorporated his former combat experiences to improve unit operations

o his vast experience and competence led to his selection over 10 other seasoned NCOs as an Advanced Cardiac Life Support Instructor

o honor graduate from the Advanced Noncommissioned Officer Course

o identified and fixed problems with truck preparation that resulted in cutting our mission prep time by 25%

o implemented a proactive program to reduce tool shortages; over 500 man hours saved in six month period

o improved Battalion supply, maintenance, and financial programs, producing a 20% increase in equipment serviceability rates

o incorporated a variety of techniques that expedited the completion of all maintenance tasks

o increased the emergency supply of blood which optimized patient care and survival

o increased production by 100% RA and 50% USAR volume over calendar year 08 o inherited a sub-standard Maintenance Control program; made improvements that exceeded Brigade standards

o instrumental in the ROTC Detachment exceeding recruitment mission by 10%

o knowledge of PDF Order-Of-Battle enhanced this unit's capabilities during Operation Desert Thrust

o knowledge, skills, and abilities equal to or greater than peers and superiors

o knowledgeable NCO who demonstrated the ability to manage numerous tasks simultaneously

o led a highly successful isolated unit 500 miles from supervision and support at Fort Bragg

o made Dean's List with distinction for 4.0 grade average in Bachelor degree program

o made decisions based upon his and his personnel's experience; always made the right choices for the team as a whole

o made the Commandant's list in BNCOC by achieving a top academic average of 99%

o maintained 100% SIDPERS rate even under arduous Operation Desert Storm conditions

o maintained a 3.0 or above grade point average

o maintained all certifications required for transition to 91W

o maintained an 90% solve rate on investigative actions; above USACIDC's goal!

o maintained SIDPERS rating of 100% for past 12 months

o makes sound decisions; takes responsibility for his actions o managed all aviation maintenance enabling his team to amass over 500 combat flight hours maintaining an OR rate of over 95%

o managed complex five-day FTX, normally a field grade officer duty; increased capabilities with zero injuries

o managed the deployment, delivery, and installation of new communications suite supporting SMDC's newest radar system

o management expertise successfully supported two maneuver Task Forces, over 1,000 Soldiers, across three provinces, the only brigade FSC tasked with this mission

o manages a Brigade Retention program which is normally a Master Sergeant duty

o mastered the JPERSTAT accounting for over 2,000 personnel and often trained the subordinate battalion S1 section on how to properly report their personnel

o maximized the use of automation; developed procedures adapted by the entire unit for admin and training

o medical knowledge and attention to detail and ability to make split-second decisions saved numerous lives

o multiplied effectiveness of medical care by dedicating off-duty hours to the care of local nationals and coalition forces

o named NCO Instructor of the Quarter over six other NCOs for 1st quarter FY09

o one of two recruiters in unit to be named "Best of the Best" in nationwide production contest

o orchestrated an efficient maintenance plan which recovered 12 UH60A aircraft upon redeployment from OEF and OIF o orchestrated the resupply of all expendable items in minimal time which was critical to the success of the unit's deployment to Baghdad

o organized internal team command maintenance program resulting in a 98% operational readiness rate for all team assigned equipment

o organized the set up and execution of an extremely successful Organizational Day

o organized, equipped, and deployed six inspection teams to the USSR

o outstanding ability to plan and direct operations and activities of any scope or size

o outstanding Battle Staff skills; key to success of platoon and company operations

o outstanding judgment; always gives sound advice and guidance

o outstanding knowledgeable and resourceful NCO

o overcame conditions and red tape to complete job when no one else would

o performed flawlessly as acting First Sergeant of NCO Academy consisting of ten BNCOC classes

o Physical Security NCO program received no deficiencies on last Command inspection

o picked as section sergeant over five other SSGs

o possesses the ability to make sound decisions with precision, accuracy, and speed

o prepared Central Material Services (CMS) for the 2010 Joint Commission on Accreditation of Healthcare Organizations (JCAHO) Survey; key to success o prioritized travel of all replacements during Operation CHOKE HOLD meeting 100% of DA requirements

o processed over 35 elimination packets with zero errors

o professional competence responsible for two battalions winning Quarterly Excellence Award for personnel

o proficient in all technical areas

o proposed, developed, and documented the revision of the CMF 51 SGM authorizations

o proved her importance to the 103d ESC's ability to successfully prepare for its war-time mission

o provided logistical advice; supervised the initial fielding of 22 trucks, ammunition, uniforms, and other MTOE to Iraqi Security Battalion

o provided critical input to the Computer Network Operations Execution Order (CNO EXORD) that was ultimately adopted by Army G3 as standard

o provided quick first aid to his crew member which saved the soldier's finger

o qualified expert with the M16A2 and SAW

o quick response and medical skills saved six soldiers' lives during Operation IRON FURY

o quickly mastered all facets of PACOM's largest distribution element, reduced workload on team

o ranked third in the FORSCOM maintenance excellence award program

o ranked third of 20 recruiters in mission accomplishment

o rated Best Wrecker Operator in the Brigade by the Commander

o received 90% rating on his Instructor Evaluations

o received a commendable rating in publications management during Brigade Organizational Inspection

o received a rating of best supply operations during second and fourth quarters FY09

o received ACOE Customer Service Excellence Award in March 2010

o received an Army Achievement Medal for his timely processing of NCOERs

o received ARCOM for Best Contract Maintenance, vehicle, during Corps Logistic Inspection

o received ARCOM for development of unit MOS library

o received award for his part in the first ever MSE deployment to FOB Falcon

o received Battalion rating of Excellence for OPFOR leader in company Field Training Exercise

o received certificate of achievement for outstanding leadership ability while attending BNCOC

o received commanding general's commendation for instructing commander and First Sergeant course

o received commendable rating as 1SG in all areas during the Battalion Command Inspection

o received commendable rating as Training NCO during Battalion CIP

o received commendable rating during annual CIP for Unit Fire Marshall duties

o received DIA commendations for his contributions to the POW-MIA National Data Base

o received excellent evaluations for all nine rotational battalions for 10 separate events o received excellent rating on NBC during Brigade Command inspection

o received five outstanding classroom evaluations during this reporting period

o received I Corps CSM coin for excellence

o received the Brigade Disciplinary Award twice for unit excellence

o received the Medical Order of Military Merit from the Surgeon General for sustained superior performance

o recognized by 23rd TAACOM CG for best concurrent training during Aerial Gunnery Exercise

o recognized by Battalion Commander as the most efficient Operations Sergeant for out processing and graduating a PLDC class

o recognized by BDE CSM for excellence as NCOIC during post Change of Command ceremonies

o recognized by Brigade Commander for excellence as NCOIC of special fitness program

o recognized by Fort Campbell CSM for excellence as a member of Post color guard during Veterans Day ceremonies

o recognized by Post Commander for professionalism of his soldiers' Squad Live Fire exercise

o recognized for outstanding performance during the Follow-on Test and Evaluation

o recognized with AAM for commendable performance during Secure Tactical Data Network IV

o recommended for the Air Medal for his calm and efficient execution of flight duties during medevac missions in support of OEF o reconstructed 15 lost promotion packets resulting in 14 promotions

o reduced Qualified Not Enlisted rate from 10 percent to all time low of 2.5 percent

o reduced waiting period for Computerized Tomography exams from 1 months to 2 days

o repeatedly called upon to work with depot MSE technicians at Tobyhanna Army Depot

o responded to 55 IEDs that the Iraq Security Forces reported; secured the surrounding area until the IEDs were neutralized

o revised and implemented the company Field Sanitation Program and SOP changing the inspected area from black to green

o revised Brigade reenlistment program, won CG's Reenlistment Trophy

o revised examination procedures for crew members, incorporated low light requirements; improved mission readiness

o saw patients, ordered supplies, including medications and completely reorganized the TMC to make it more efficient for providing emergency trauma care

o scored 95 on latest SQT, a significant improvement

o scored a perfect score of 1000 points on Tank Table VIII as Tank Commander

o selected above peers for difficult missions

o selected from among peers to act as 1SG

o selected ahead of peers to attend PLDC

o selected as assistant platoon sergeant over 11 other NCOs

o selected as Battalion Master Dragon Gunner for two consecutive quarters

o selected as Distinguished Honor Graduate for BNCOC, Fort Sill, Oklahoma

o selected as Guidance Counselor of the Year for CY08

o selected as Platoon Sergeant; a Sergeant First Class position

o selected by scuba team to train 1st Group pre-scuba course

o selected for a special mission at Battalion level over 5 other crew chiefs

o selected for evaluation and verification of technical manuals at contractor level

o selected for induction into the Sergeant Morales Club

o selected for outstanding Public Service Award for 2000

o selected for promotion to Sergeant First Class from the secondary zone

o selected from among 150 other NCOs as National Defense Transportation Association NCO of the Year

o selected from among peers to become the Army's first C-20 flight engineer

o selected over 22 SFCs to be the Senior Instructor of Jumpmaster Branch

o selected over more senior noncommissioned officers to fill CW2 position

o selected over peers to be cross-trained for the next Motor Sergeant position

o selected over peers to perform in SSG position

o selected to compete at DA level in the Phillip A. Connelly Competition for small dining facility o selected to perform duties as Platoon Sergeant; obtained excellent results

o selected to represent the 3rd Ranger Training Battalion in the Best Ranger Competition

o selected to train the Royal Saudi Air Defense Force during Desert Storm

o self-motivated; committed to excellence

o self-starter; displays a high degree of initiative

o served as convoy commander for over 150 Combat Logistic Patrols with no loss of Soldiers or equipment

o served as the senior medical advisor in support of tactical convoy operations and close quarters combat live fire ranges during OIF II

o set the standard within the Brigade for Range certification

o sought self-improvement through correspondence courses while deployed during OIF II

o spearheaded renovation of over twenty B-HUTs, with limited time and resources, to accommodate living area shortages for brigade personnel

o spent many hours of self-study to improve job skills

o stood up a Fuel & Electric Section which was fully operational in three months

o successfully conducted three theater retrograde missions, one being the largest retrograde ever conducted in theater

o successfully established and managed Class IV supplies needed for repair operations in the BDE LSA foot print at Bagram Air Base, Afghanistan

o supervised the processing of 1,000 military police reports with zero errors o supported over a dozen named missions with intelligence that identified the most likely avenues of enemy approach

o surpassed the Brigade's retention goals by 50%

o tackled training, planning, and communications problems that threatened unit mission; ensured 100% reliable comm

o tactfully managed problems of leading a Task Force of over 300 US and Italian soldiers

o task oriented and detail minded; completes assignments to the fullest while staying focused on goal

o technical and tactical expertise led to his assignment to the company-level Quality Control section

o technically and tactically proficient

o technically and tactically proficient Master Gunner; supervised over 200 ranges and qualifications across the brigade

o technically competent NCO; best I've known in my 15 years of service

o the only Soldier to consistently perform daily checks

o total competence in the areas of security and theater specific requirements

o two time Brigade NCO of the Quarter

o unafraid of making decisions despite personal risk

o unique and comprehensive computer skills

o unparalleled ability to multitask and achieve outstanding results

o used initiative and skill to tackle and complete complex missions

o very resourceful and innovative NCO

o vital asset for the platoon; knowledgeable and persistent

o volunteered for platoon sergeant position and was accepted over several more senior NCOs

o was first to identify malaria as common ailment at sick call and threat to operations in Senegal

o won five gold and two silver medals at the division level culinary arts competition

o won highly competitive mentorship award from Federally Employed Women, Pacific Region

o won Recruiter of the Year FY08

o won Soldier of the Year, Ft Lewis, Washington

o won the daily Barracks and Maintenance Inspections Award

o won the Fort Sheridan land navigation course competition

o won Third Region Soldier of the Year Competition

o wrote and implemented NCODP SOP which is now USAMA's standard program

o wrote the SMU DSN directory, an invaluable tactical reference used by deployed units around the world

Needs Improvement (Competence)

o consistently underperformed, jeopardizing the safety and security of the entire unit

o performed admirably in most duties but needs to concentrate on qualification

o when reminded, can be a very productive Specialist, requires supervision

o a capable Soldier but fails to use his abilities to the fullest

o not focused, often distracted, her accuracy rate was the lowest in the shop

o failed to comply with instructions of superiors on several occasions

o an outstanding technical resource but needs to work on tact and communications skills

o his performance was often inaccurate but wildly incorrect when under stress

o failed to use time wisely; consistently failed to meet administrative suspense

o did not always make the effort required to become proficient in her duties

o performance is sometimes above average but erratic and undependable

o did not meet expectations in...

o requires additional time to prepare for courses

o needs to increase technical abilities in...

o is indifferent to suggestions for advancement and misses many opportunities for improvement o demonstrated lack of ability to execute his duties and depends on others for help

o was unable to qualify in key tasks and limited the readiness of the entire team

o performed admirably in most duties but needs to concentrate on leadership

o failure to use TM is a frequent problem and risks equipment and personnel

o performance does not meet standards; work with supervisor to address areas of timeliness and responsibility

o performance needs improvement in order to maintain career goals

o as SFC and manager, no longer a mechanic, concentrate on developing staff skills

o recommend increased study and practice in order to meet performance goals

o not meeting responsibilities to peers; focus on task qualification or risk reassignment

Physical Fitness & Military Bearing

Physical fitness is the physical and mental ability to accomplish the mission. Total fitness includes weight control, smoking cessation, control of substance abuse, stress management, and physical training. It covers strength, endurance, stamina, flexibility, speed, agility, coordination, and balance. NCOs are responsible for their own physical fitness and that of their subordinates.

Military bearing consists of posture, dress, and overall appearance. Bearing also includes an outward display of confidence and enthusiasm and a respect for military protocol. While all Soldiers are expected to present a military image, Leaders are expected to make on-the-spot corrections to peers and subordinates.

o a model Soldier; sharp military bearing and pride in service

o agile! Accomplished combat operations dismounted, by air, and in HMMWVs

o always displays a commendable military appearance

o always prepared to go the distance

o an example of modest and capable leadership

o appearance above reproach; displays positive image for soldiers to emulate

o appearance always immaculate; exceptional role model for soldiers

o appearance and bearing above reproach

o appearance and military bearing were flawless

o aspiring performer; sets and achieves high standards

o assisted squad in averaging 270 on APFT score

o awarded Div Coin from CG, 82nd Airborne Div for uniform appearance during the annual inspection

o bearing and appearance above reproach

o bearing and appearance are exemplary

o built strong relationship with locals by involving them in daily fitness improvement programs

o can adjust to any situation

o carried out three improvement projects valued at over $3M; strengthened relations between Coalition Forces and Iraqi citizens

o coach and starting player for 1st place basketball team

o competed and consistently placed 1st with battalion cross country team

o completed a physically demanding ascent to the summit of Mt Fuji, 21,500 feet

o confident and mentally sharp NCO

o confident, sharp looking NCO

o consistent high standards for personal appearance; enforced those standards in NCOs and Soldiers

o consistently demonstrated sound physical and mental toughness

o consistently displayed a positive attitude and high level of confidence

o consistently displays a positive mental attitude

o consistently scored 270 and above on APFT test

o consistently set the example for soldiers to follow

o constantly strove to strengthen and refine his professional effectiveness o crisp military bearing represents an equally impressive performance

o dedicated to fitness; motivates others to exceed standards

o dedicated to the mission and places high emphasis on mission-related tasks

o deliberate planning and practice produced admirable results

o delivered stellar results after rigorous training regimen

o demands and enforces high standards of his soldiers' appearance

o demonstrated positive mental outlook; always gives 100 percent

o demonstrated stamina and will to survive at JRTC

o demonstrated what could be accomplished; responsible for the entire section's increased scores

o designed platoon PT program; now used as company standard

o developed a demanding PT program for his platoon

o developed a PT program for the staff which improved each score by at least 25 points

o dignified in presence and appearance

o disciplined in attitude, appearance, poise and authority

o displayed mental toughness under extreme pressure

o displayed tremendous physical attributes during NTC

o displays a strong sense of pride in the uniform

o displays impressive poise under stress

o distinguished Honor Graduate of Master Fitness Trainer Course o earned Post Athlete of the Year through unparalleled effort and resolve

o encourages soldiers to seek self-improvement

o endurance is unmatched, leads platoon in two-mile run

o established Brigade Physical fitness Program; improved unit strength and readiness

o exceeded APFT and unit physical standards with ease

o exceeded standards for appearance and bearing

o exceeds all standards of physical fitness

o excellent mental and physical abilities; displayed strong stamina

o excellent physical abilities and bearing

o excellent physical condition; led advanced PT during physical training

o excellent role model in bearing and appearance

o excellent runner, ran two miles in 12 minutes

o excellent swimmer; taught Tarzan how to swim

o exhibited strong mental flexibility and confidence

o exhibited exemplary military appearance

o finished first in class 10K division run

o forged strong commitment to fitness

o fully committed to success; always gives 100%

o functions well under stress

o graduated Ranger, Airborne, Air Assault, and Combat Leaders courses at 40 years of age

o great physical and mental endurance

o hand-picked to run the Master Fitness Program for the battalion

o hand-picked to march as a member of the USAREUR Honor Guard

o helped his clinic win the Commanders Trophy for APFT Excellence for the third consecutive quarter

o her impressive fitness scores encouraged peers to increase their efforts

o her mental toughness and bearing were beyond reproach

o highly disciplined soldier in all aspects of bearing and appearance

o highly motivated; a way out front leader

o his example is responsible for the fitness improvement of the entire team

o his mental toughness and discipline brought him to new found physical goals

o his platoon averaged 290 points on the APFT due to his training

o impeccable appearance; role model standard

o impeccable military bearing

o impressed peers with PT test results, inspired all shop members to redouble their efforts

o impressive military appearance and bearing

o improved physical performance through diligent rehearsals

o improved APFT score 30% over last year; outstanding effort!

o incorporated plan which ultimately raised the unit APFT score by 15 percent o increased APFT score by 65 points during this rating period

o inspired self-improvement in subordinates through sterling personal example

o instills confidence and pride in soldiers through mentoring

o is alert, quick, and responsive

o leads battalion in endurance and two-mile run

o led company marathon relay to a first and second place finish

o maintained a positive attitude and deep pride in mission accomplishment

o maintained excellent physical fitness; encourages the same standards in others

o maintained professional bearing in relations with new second lieutenants

o maintains his military bearing at all times

o Master Fitness Trainer; served as unit instructor for daily PT

o mature, well-rounded leader; inspires trust and teamwork

o meets height and weight requirements of AR 600-9

o mentally and physically fit to handle any task

o mentally quick and resourceful

o mentally tough; able to manage numerous tasks at one time

o mentally, physically, and emotionally ready to lead in combat

o military bearing, tact, and performance were at a level well beyond his pay grade o motivated platoon to achieve 100% first time go rate on APFT

o motivated platoon to improve PT average by 30 points

o motivated Soldiers to excel during company APFT with an average score over 290; fostered teamwork and esprit de corps within his team

o motivated, enthusiastic NCO who took lead in organized physical fitness training of all soldiers

o motivated, enthusiastic NCO; took lead in unit fitness training

o motivates the unit by giving challenging physical fitness training

o never backs down from a challenge

o obtained a passing score on his APFT

o one of only 13 to complete arduous 13K Mountain Run on FOB Thunder

o outstanding endurance; sustained combat operations in a hostile environment outside of the FOB for 72 hours straight

o outstanding role model for noncommissioned officers

o performs well under pressure

o physically challenged his subordinates to exceed standards

o physically fit soldier with strong stamina

o physically fit, scored 300 on most recent APFT

o physically tough and mentally strong

o placed first in weight division in the 2009 Fort Sill Bodybuilding Contest

o platoon achieved 100% first time pass rate on APFT for two consecutive testing cycles o positive mental outlook and attitude

o possesses mental and physical stamina to go the distance

o possesses the stamina and will to continue when others stop

o possesses unparalleled bearing and presence

o practiced continually, efforts paid off; most fit in section

o praised by the BDE CSM for service as Master Fitness Trainer and the Aquatic PT program instructor

o presented a professional, soldierly appearance at all times

o presents a healthy, strong and confident demeanor

o pride and purpose are evident in his demeanor

o produced highest battery score in Battalion

o professional manner, commanding presence, and dominant personality

o projected enthusiasm and confidence when assisting Soldiers

o projected excellent military bearing and appearance

o projected self-confidence, authority, and purpose

o promoted platoon fitness by leading by example

o radiates strength and ability

o raised platoon APFT average by 24 points

o raised the section PT score by 20%

o received 1st and second place in three inter-service weight lifting events

o recognized by Battalion Commander for being an outstanding role model

o rehabilitated injured knee and won Physical Fitness Badge

o remains calm and poised under pressure

o remains flexible and cooperative under all conditions

o responsible for subordinates' fitness, led squad to a 280 APFT average

o scored over 280 on last two APFTs

o selected as MVP for base level softball team

o selected as USAREUR Athlete of the Year 07

o selected for and competed with the Women's Basketball Team, won second place, USAREUR

o selected NCO of the Quarter

o selected Tobyhanna Army Depot's Athlete of the Year

o sets laudable example for subordinates

o sets the standard by which excellence is measured

o sharp appearance is commendable

o showed what could be accomplished with practice and effort; encouraged peers to follow example

o singled out by several Army Aviation Officers for his technical competence and desire to teach others

o Soldier's professional guidance and leadership has led to the ideal example of a soldier and leader to all of first squad

o solely responsible for platoon APFT average rising from 210 to 230

o strong stamina and will to win

o successfully completed the Army Air Assault School

o supported all Commander's Cup sports events

o took extreme pride in personal appearance

o trained platoon to exceed Brigade standards of fitness

o unquestionable physical stamina

o volunteered for the 2008 Para-Olympic law enforcement run from Leesville to Alexandria covering over 25 miles

o was Post racquetball Championship runner-up

o well-disciplined soldier; displayed the utmost in bearing and appearance

o well-rounded leader; inspires teamwork and trust

o won 2008 American Drug Free Power lifting Association Men's National Competition

o won first place in battalion physical fitness competition with extended APFT score of 300

Needs Improvement (Fitness & Military Bearing)

o made remarkable progress in aerobic fitness but still approaching minimum standards in...

o presents sharp military appearance but needs to realize importance of subtlety

o counseled twice for disrespect toward an NCO; need to focus on relationship skills

o refused suggestions to attend counseling until his problems escalated to the point of making him unfit for duty

o failed to meet APFT standards for the two mile run and sit-ups with a total score of 124

o doesn't realize the critical importance of following orders and may endanger this battalion

o was disciplined for assault and his off-duty actions make him unfit for duty

o superb performance but uniform and bearing do not meet standards and will hold this Soldier back

o presents an unprofessional appearance and lacks military bearing

o complained about time spent in the field and deployments; adversely affected morale and discipline

o lacks respect for chain of command and needs improvement in peer communications

o displayed a consistent lack of initiative and enthusiasm and is the subject of frequent counseling

o failed to render the proper respect and was subject to non-judicial punishment twice o has not made any effort to change his behavior during this reporting period and is not fit for retention

o made substantial progress in qualification but failure to follow instructions limited efforts

o needs improvement in push- ups, all other areas exemplary

o need to focus on uniform; must be clean and serviceable at all times

o encouraged section to collaborate in response to questioning and obstructed investigation which hindered results

o remember to show proper respect to NCOs and use tact when communicating with peers and other units

o improve example to troops by demonstrating patience and respect for others

o performance above average but not enough attention paid to supervisory duties

o must increase supervision and training of subordinates or risk reduction in mission effectiveness

o lacked empathy when providing guidance or training

o should encourage team to exceed standards not just meet them to keep level of achievement high

o concentrate on assigned tasks and meeting assigned responsibility before assisting other squads

o finish assigned work before volunteering to participate in HQ events

o made sports participation priority and repeatedly left tasks to teammates and now qualification is questionable

o undependable and left responsibility for completing assigned tasks to coworkers so often that now he is not qualified on any task o has lowest on-time reporting rate but highest rate of participation in Battalion sports, needs to give more attention to duties

o encouraged peers to reduce their efforts to avoid being exposed for not performing his duties

o spent inordinate amount of time on phone, should realize work is the priority and personal calls are limited to 5 minutes a day

o often unavailable for scheduled work but never failed to discipline subordinates for tardiness; should set the example for Soldiers

o avoided deployment by emphasizing undocumented physical and domestic problems at the expense of his section

o provided limited support to team; always last in and first to leave due to child care responsibilities, places self above squad

o treated subordinates harshly, should develop more empathy for troops, make effort to understand their circumstances

o failed to follow up and ensure subordinates participated in regular PT; PT results for section worst ever

o failed to properly train his Soldiers in physical training, resulting in their failure of the APFT

Leadership

Leadership is influencing others to accomplish the mission. It includes setting tough but achievable standards and requiring that they be met. It means sincerely caring for subordinates and their families, conducting honest, constructive counseling, and setting the example by word and act. A major component of leadership is humility, sacrifice, and a sense of fairness.

o 95% of the battalion's CMF11 soldiers earned EIB, a tremendous logistics effort!

o a firm, resolute leader; exemplifies the ideal leader

o a prompt and diligent administrator

o a real leader, gives 110 percent; demands soldiers' best and looks out for their welfare

o a role model and mentor for other drill sergeants

o a true mission-oriented leader

o accomplished the harder right instead of the easier wrong

o achieved 100% enrollment in continuing education courses among members of his section

o action-oriented manager who fostered a war-fighting attitude in his Soldiers

o actively leads AIT soldiers physical development and trains to excel in common task skills

o addressed and corrected long-standing relationship issues with sister units and Headquarters

o advanced through duty positions as Survey Team Member, Survey Team Chief, and finally NCOIC during his assignment here o always contributes 110 percent to team effort

o always placed mission first; unquestionable devotion to duty

o always put soldiers' needs first

o an effective Supply Sergeant, tailors her leadership style to the task at hand

o an exceptional leader, manager, and organizer

o assembled and trained an RSOP team; facilitated rapid site deployment and ensured Table VIII Gunnery success

o assisted with building two new brigades over the past six months; expanded capability while maintaining current strength

o awarded Bronze Star by Division Commander for leadership during Desert Storm

o awarded CAB for actions and leadership as Tower Guard during attack of assigned tower in March 2009

o barracks selected as the Post representative in the TRADOC Community of Excellence Competition

o battalion awarded Commanding General's award for reenlistment

o battalion Color Guard recognized as outstanding by the FORSCOM Command Sergeant Major

o battalion command inspectors rated his equipment and shop as best in the battalion

o battery finished first in Battalion individual skills competition in Saudi Arabia

o best Fire Direction Center section in the battery during platoon ARTEPs o cadets under his charge won their division in the National Parachute Competition

o captured Best in Brigade through diligent preparation, practice, and hard work

o carefully and objectively assessed problems through sound analytical process

o cares for soldiers; benefited both them and our unit

o catalyst for excellence during the FY10 Command Inspection, 5 areas were rated as outstanding

o CG noted Battalion as outstanding during Division ARTEP

o chosen as switching supervisor over numerous qualified SFCs

o chosen by Brigade and Battalion Commanders to lead reconnaissance of attack routes at CMTC

o chosen over seven Sergeants First Class for Operation Soldier Assignment

o chosen to brief and demonstrate the M-1 howitzer to foreign dignitaries

o chosen to serve as acting Brigade Command Sergeant Major for a period of six weeks

o coached and motivated 5 soldiers to win Soldier/NCO boards and produced one PLDC Honor Graduate

o coached battalion biathlon team which won division

o coached green National Guard unit to pass first readiness evaluation; ready for deployment

o coached Service Rifle Team to victory in the inter-service championships

o coached Soldiers to seize both Battalion NCO and Soldier of the Quarter o coached Charlie Battery to a first place finish during a Brigade Quarterly Maintenance Inspection

o commendable performance as acting commander for three months during Commander's absence

o commended by 23rd TAACOM CSM for improving quality of life, barracks for single Soldiers

o committed NCO that lives by "Mission first, Soldiers always"

o committed to providing the best quality of life and training for soldiers

o completed physically challenging competitions in the 911 Memorial Run, the Army Ten Miler and the Marine Corps Marathon

o conducted professional development for 5 NCOs

o consistently developed new ways to measure results, improve SOP development; ensured Iraqi Security Forces had a practical foundation to build upon

o consistently leads from the front in training

o constantly stressed mission and readiness

o continued to complete his duties as Platoon Sergeant while serving as Acting First Sergeant

o coordinated and developed a $110K renovation project to upgrade a major dining facility and increase capacity

o coordinated over $3 million in transportation costs to move 2nd BDE Task Force successfully to JRTC

o corrected behavior that caused relationship problems with Headquarters and sister units

o counseled 25 students during rating period, 100% graduated, 3 with honors o dedicated to the betterment of peers and subordinates, a selfless leader

o delivered a deployment-ready team on time despite budget and training shortfalls

o demanded the best training environment for soldiers; accepted nothing less than sincere effort and quality results

o demonstrated a can-do attitude and level of optimism beyond his peers

o demonstrated outstanding comprehension and leadership skills as team chief

o demonstrated sincere care for soldiers by inspiring and developing performance through on-the-spot counseling

o demonstrated sound and mature judgment

o deployed to Exercise Cold Response '10 with temperatures below -30 Celsius with no cold weather injuries

o designed and implemented a PAC training team, improved soldier actions timeliness by 20%

o developed and published the first Stryker Battalion TACSOP which was adopted as the brigade standard

o developed creative and effective management initiatives

o developed fire mission scheduling system that reduced fire support response time by 5 minutes

o developed outstanding command retention program, excellent results for FY05, cited best in the MACOM

o developed soldiers through positive counseling, coaching, and mentoring

o developed two previously marginal dining facilities into Connelly Cup finalists

o devoted after hours to resolving Soldier problems

o devoted all his time and effort to the success of his platoon

o Dining Facility received a 1st Place rating from the Health Promotion Council; first in four years!

o directed the efforts of HHC in becoming the FORSCOM Maintenance Excellence Award Winner

o directly responsible for A Company seizing "Top Gun" in Division during TT VIII

o directly responsible for supervising the unit's orderly room; received commendable rating during CI

o displayed a strong concern for soldiers; effectively assisted in working through their problems using base resources

o displayed a genuine concern for soldiers

o distinguished himself as ahead of his peers with initiative and unmatched technical expertise

o distinguished himself as both the acting Senior Drill Sergeant and acting First Sergeant

o distinguished his Bradley team on TT VIII during Level II Gunnery with a perfect score of 1000 points

o distinguished squad as TOP GUN in battalion during Annual Service Practice at McGregor Range

o driving force in battalion attaining a 75% pass rate on EIB, the highest in all of Afghanistan

o during an attack at NTC, he led the remnants of three scattered platoons and secured the objective

o earned the Army Commendation Medal for his comprehensive Soldier Handbook

o earned the respect and admiration of his entire platoon and Battalion peers

o earned this station the Eastern Sector "Best Facility Award" o effectively led and inspired sub-standard soldiers to willingly raise performance to Army standards

o efficiently deployed all of the battalion's staff sections, personnel, and equipment from home station to Iraq without incident or injury

o enrolled every Soldier in his platoon in the CLEP Program to earn college credit

o ensured 100% of assigned personnel qualified on individual and crew served weapons with over 50% qualifying as expert

o ensured Soldier morale, discipline, SOP standards, and Army regulations were upheld in the absence of the First Sergeant

o ensured that his soldiers and assigned civilian translators were treated as equals; everyone was mission critical

o established and developed an unprecedented atmosphere of pride and professionalism

o exceeded the Battalion standard; he trained four soldiers to achieve an average score of 280

o executed first ever FTX for MACOM HHC

o exemplifies initiative, leadership, and devotion to duty

o facilitated platoon's advancement in qualification through meticulous scheduling

o facilities under his supervision were awarded TRADOC's Best Classroom Facilities

o flawlessly supervised medical treatment during Operation ENDURING FREEDOM-PHILIPPINES in Mindanao, Southern Philippines

o fostered high morale and a total winning attitude and spirit

o fostered teamwork and esprit de corps within his section

o gained working knowledge of local language in order to facilitate effective communication between Soldiers and Afghan Local Nationals

o gave 100% loyalty and support to chain of command

o gives loyalty and leadership support to the chain of command

o guidance and training programs improved SQT scores by 15% to a 90 average with zero failures

o guided new 2LTs through complex information project, received commander's approval for efforts

o guided, motivated, and tutored two Soldiers who ultimately won Battalion NCO of the Quarter

o has outstanding rapport with subordinates and is able to extract the most from each individual by tailoring leadership to the task at hand

o has strong leadership attributes, encouraged his team to achieve best repair rate in SWA

o her managerial skills and attention to detail pushed our clinic to win the Access to Care award for 2 consecutive years

o his ammunition squad was named the best in the history of AH-64A Helicopter Fielding

o his devotion to duty is always evident

o his dynamic leadership promised and delivered the brigade overall RE-UP awards two years straight

o his efforts helped to produce the winner of the Regimental Gavin Squad competition

o his guidance produced a MACOM Connelly winner in Best Field Kitchen competition

o his leadership and experience ensured the battalion won the USAREUR Supply Excellence Award o his leadership resulted in an excellent rating on the AMC IG with four commendables in Soldier support

o his leadership was the main factor in the company obtaining brigade-high 90% 11 series SQT average

o his leadership yielded the highest readiness rate for a V Corps unit

o his newspaper was rated as MACOM best in Keith L. Ware competition

o his platoon earned the Distinguished Marching Unit designation for excellence in drill and ceremonies

o his platoon rifle marksmanship program resulted in 18 experts out of 24 personnel

o his platoon survival rate for NTC battles was 90%, highest in the OPFOR Regiment

o his Radio Team won the Brigade and III Corps Artillery Communications Competition

o his squad successfully assaulted and defended key facilities during the Helmand Province Campaign

o his training produced a TOC operated solely by NCOs for Key Resolve '08

o identified motivation problems, corrected, produced incalculable savings in time and money

o implemented a physical training program which increased platoon's APFT average from 245 to 265 while deployed

o implemented a maintenance program that increased the ICP Brigade's overall operational readiness rate from 20% to over 80% in only 6 months

o implemented training program to increase leaders' confidence as Convoy Protection Platform Commanders o improved unit morale by organizing and leading trips for entire unit and family members

o in 12 months, four of his recruiters earned the Recruiter Ring, the Command's highest award

o in the absence of an officer, assumed command of the detachment during two separate missions at JRTC

o influenced and mentored his two soldiers to complete Warrior leader Course; one made the Commandant's list

o influenced Soldiers to accomplish all assigned missions

o inspired 31B IET soldiers to break Post 9mm Qualification Record with 99% 1st time GOs

o inspired NCOs to excellence; 24 soldiers received the CINC EUSA Distinguished Leadership Award

o inspired soldier in her platoon to achieve Soldier of the Year honors

o inspired team to win top medic team in the Army during the 6th annual Expert Field Medical Competition

o inspired three soldiers to compete and win Post NCO of the quarter

o inspired unit to consistently exceed training standards

o inspired self-improvement in subordinates

o instilled a mission-first attitude; motivated entire unit to do the same

o instilled a sense of pride in Soldiers

o instilled discipline in his unit; led the battalion with the least amount of discipline problems during rating period

o instructed Soldiers in guarding Local Nationals, ensured thorough knowledge of Escalation of Force while providing considerate and fair treatment o instrumental in one Soldier winning the Brigade Soldier of the Year competition and two Soldiers winning the Battalion Soldier of the Quarter Board

o introduced training and evaluation in preparation for MOS realignment; responsible for successful transition

o knowledge, experience, and military bearing make him a role model NCO

o leadership was paramount in Battalion winning US Army Air Traffic Control Battalion of the Year

o leading by example has encouraged individual growth and responsibility

o leads by example, led team into Iraq to rescue an Air Force member during Operation Desert Storm

o leads by example; doesn't abuse authority

o led and inspired marginal Soldiers to practice, perform, and succeed

o led by example while executing over 22 challenging combat missions; conducted thorough Pre-Combat Inspections to ensure his Soldiers were always ready

o led division to win TRADOC Commanders Trophy for Best Outdoor Training Facility

o led company to first place standing in Ft Bragg Commanders Cup intramural sports competition

o led redeployment of over 200 Soldiers and 55 vehicles by air, land, and sea; innovative contract saved $100K

o led his men to beat four of six rifle squads in a Company Biathlon on Camp Zama, Japan

o led his section to repel two attacks against Iraqi Security Forces during the Al-Ghadir holiday o led NCO trainers during Expert Field Medical Badge training yielding a remarkable 70% pass rate

o led inexperienced platoon to achieve a 100% first time GO on M-16 qualification

o led platoon to Distinguished Marksmanship honors during annual battalion shooting competition

o led platoon to highest APFT average in Battalion

o led this unit to exceed standards for operations during Brigade Command Inspection

o lives by the leadership attributes of be, know, do

o made Commandant's List while attending Basic Noncommissioned Officers Course

o made well informed decisions; provided his Soldiers with an environment conducive to effective training

o maintained a daily physical fitness regimen in forward deployed theater despite increased workload

o maintained the late NCO-ER rate at zero percent for nine consecutive months

o maintenance section received a distinguished rating for security operations at NTC rotation 09/01

o major factor behind reenlistment program being Best in Size category for 5th Signal Command

o maneuvered forklift through insurgent territory to emplace force protection barriers with precision, reclaimed front line; contributed to TF Tiger Mission success

o meets challenges head on; displays courage, conviction, and professionalism at all times

o mentored and trained Soldier who won Soldier of the Month and Soldier of the Quarter o mentored one NCO who was nominated for membership in the Sergeant Audie Murphy Club

o mentored only Soldier to become I Corp PLDC honor graduate

o mentorship produced two consecutive MACOM Soldier of the Year winners

o mission accomplishment, care of Soldiers, and leading by example are his priorities

o motivated 55 Retention NCOs throughout Korea to achieve the top retention rate in the Army

o motivated her section to perform to the best of their abilities

o motivated his entire section to qualify expert with the 60mm mortar

o motivated his Soldiers to perform to the best of their ability as individuals and as a team

o motivated Soldiers to excel during company APFT with an average score over 290

o motivated Soldiers to take on tough missions and achieve success

o motivated squad to place first in the 11 mile road march during company level competition

o motivated others to achieve and exceed unit goals

o noted by AADC Inspector General as having the best Sergeants' Time program in AADC

o ensured all brigade ammunition managers were prepared for the 1ID Inspection through rigorous self-inspections and training; resulted in commendable rating

o orienteered for team on a 20 mile night road march to place second of twenty teams o out front leader; puts forth the effort to ensure mission accomplishment

o outstanding as a squad leader; an E-6 position

o outstanding leader; implemented several training programs within the company which increased readiness

o outstanding motivator of Soldiers; gets superior results

o outstanding motivator; inspired platoon to consistently exceed standards

o outstanding NCODP program; proven by company accomplishing all 10 missions at NTC

o oversaw the execution of over 100 Military Police combat missions in Iraq without any loss of life or equipment

o oversaw weaponry training program which resulted in a 30% increase in overall unit marksmanship

o performed commendably for 6 months as a Staff Sergeant in a Sergeant First Class position

o performed duties as acting First Sergeant

o performed duties as First Sergeant; obtained excellent results!

o performed exceptionally well while leading Soldiers in difficult, constantly changing combat environment

o performed leadership tasks in a decisive and positive manner with exceptional results

o personal commitment to preparation resulted in S-4 receiving commendable ratings in all areas during the last BCI

o personal dedication to reenlistment efforts contributed to the highest QPA in Brigade o personally developed a dental tracking program that reduced deployment delays due to dental by 35%

o placed mission first; totally devoted to duty

o planned and organized an Army Emergency Relief marathon; collected over $900 for charity

o planned and executed four fund raisers which earned over $2000 for Soldier charities

o planned and implemented consistent standards required at all permanent Forward Operating Bases

o planner-manager won 2007 FORSCOM Commander's Award "Best in FORSCOM" for barracks and Overall Appearance

o platoon awarded Battalion CTT Award for Excellence; highest pass rate in 5 years

o platoon recognized by Battalion Commander for quality of training presented to AIT students

o platoon was recognized as "the best they have seen OCONUS" by the CMTC observers

o played a positive leadership role in managing a diverse section that included remote Soldiers, medics, and admin and supply personnel

o prepared seven personnel for PLDC resulting in 2 Honor Graduates and 2 Soldiers on the Commandant's List

o produced the first military music ensemble performance at the University of Rochester

o produced two quarterly and four monthly High Mileage Award winners during OIF III

o promoted harmony and teamwork; a gifted supervisor

o promoted teamwork at all levels of logistical operations within the Task Force o provided one on one training to Soldiers lagging behind peers

o provided outstanding support, even in stressful leadership situations

o puts the Army, the mission, and subordinates first before his own interests

o raised the rating of an inherited supply section from unsatisfactory to commendable within a month for the BN CIP

o received Best Team rating during JRTC as a direct result of his leadership and dedicated efforts

o received commendation from the Brigade CSM for his soldiers' appearance and performance during company BCI

o received Army Achievement Medal for leadership excellence during Post CSM's retirement review

o recognized by the Battalion Commander for leadership while conducting combat operations against terrorist network

o recognized in writing by the Airborne Association leadership for organizing the finest reunion in memory

o reduced his team's delinquency rate by 50%

o reduced test equipment calibration turn-around time from 3 days average to 1.5 days

o repeatedly demonstrated exceptional leadership and initiative

o researched, developed, and implemented an OJT program for workcenter personnel; increased task coverage to 100%

o responsible for ten of the section's 20 mechanics earning the Expert Mechanics Badge o responsible for the success of the first-ever combined special forces US-Philippines training exercise

o rewrote and published a 100 page USAREUR TACSOP during six month contingency TDY to Patch Barracks

o risked injury to save 804A generator during a fuel-fed fire; prevented $1M loss of equipment and readiness

o routinely consulted by other NCOs for advice and guidance

o sacrificed personal goals to ensure unit's mission accomplishment

o selected as Drill Sergeant of the Cycle

o selected by commander to perform high profile and difficult tasks

o selected for 1SG position over two other SFC

o selected to serve as CSM for over 500 soldiers during NTC rotation 08-04

o selected to serve as unit 1SG during highly successful NTC rotation; received commendable comments from HQ

o self-sacrificing; a real team player

o set high standards for conduct and performance

o set leadership example for peers; selected and readily accepted as platoon sergeant

o set strict but achievable standards for his Soldiers

o set the example for acceptable performance by treating local nationals and detainees with dignity and respect

o sets stringent standards and promotes excellence

o sets tough yet achievable performance standards for subordinates o sets the example for leadership; not only within his platoon, but the entire battalion

o shares responsibility for success of Fort Gordon's BOSS program; ranked 10th out of 65 other CONUS installations

o showed superior leadership by training and mentoring soldiers for deployment and continuously offered his experience and skills to those in need

o solid leader, genuinely cares for Soldiers; motivates them to accomplish all missions

o sought perfection; accomplished all duties with great accuracy and timeliness

o sound management style and procedures inspire peers and subordinates

o spreads infectious enthusiasm, improved morale

o squad consistently won gunner/squad competition within platoon

o squad ranked 1st of 15 during Battalion home station gunnery evaluation (Battle Drills)

o squad received 100% rating in last battalion ARTEP

o squad repelled enemy attack of two platoons and enabled the company to accomplish mission at CMTC

o squad was selected #1 of six squads to represent unit in the Infantry Skills Competition

o stepped up to additional responsibility of managing the multimillion dollar Voice of America Transmitter Site while the Station Manager was on leave

o stern but fair NCO who consistently exceeded established standards and demanded excellence from his subordinates

o stood up the 155th Iraqi Civil Defense Corps Bn in preparation for scheduled transfer of authority o successfully revised deployment procedures, reduced delays by 50%

o superior leadership qualities; leads by example

o supervised 55 enlisted personnel at four remote clinics located up to 5 miles away from the main hospital

o supervised and instructed four Soldiers and ten Afghan Local Nationals contracted to perform construction projects

o supervised installation's power production resulting in 3 DA and FORSCOM awards for excellence

o supervised PT program; 285 platoon average!

o supported the division-level Warfighter training events; 100% equipment delivered, 100% task rehearsal

o tactful leader and motivator with ability to successfully communicate and overcome challenges

o takes charge; a real no-nonsense leader

o the driving force in the SIDPERS section receiving a Commendable rating

o took an inherited unsatisfactory section to a commendable rating at JRTC

o took command of a failing station and led it from 50% accomplishment rate to over 100%

o trained and deployed half the team as a separate unit and then quickly integrated with other unit members; a true team player

o trained Brigade Maintenance Officer on maintenance reporting and supervised him while he trained his maintenance staff

o trained section well; scored over 1025 points out of a possible 1200 on the howitzer section evaluation o trained soldiers to perform as a cohesive team

o treats Soldiers firmly but in a manner that instills esprit de corps and unity; Soldiers work as an unstoppable team

o trusted by Commander to oversee operations in his absence

o turned the EOD school around by greatly increasing quota utilization and reducing attrition by 25%

o two of the last four Soldiers of the Month were from her section

o united a team of active duty, reserve, and National Guard soldiers into one cohesive team focused on same target

o unparalleled ability to motivate soldiers

o unparalleled ability to multitask and achieve outstanding results

o volunteered for every combat mission assigned to 2nd BN during Operation Anvil Fury

o was recognized as having the best squad at JRTC

o willingly shared his experience and insight; prepared Soldiers for future deployments and contingency operations

o won Battalion Commander's Leadership Award

o won Commanding General's Best Cooks Award for second quarter FY10

o won Honor Platoon with a platoon average of 95% in all End of Course areas

o won MACOM retention excellence award for 1 ID

Needs Improvement (Leadership)

o does not use his free time to improve his knowledge of his MOS to become a more efficient and better leader

o had to be constantly reminded to counsel and mentor Soldiers on a regular basis

o is a positive and effective leader but may need more experience before...

o exhibited strong ability to lead, should now focus on staff skills and communication

o is sometimes unaware of operational picture and often leaves subordinates unsupervised

o needs to realize importance of tact when questioning orders and effect on platoon

o leadership and managerial skills need improvement to qualify for next rank

o had poor rapport with his subordinates and was ineffectual in supervision or delegation of responsibilities

o lagged behind contemporaries in...

o an ineffective leader; overdue for ANCOC

o failed to live up to obligations

o was ineffective and provided no useful guidance

o failed to maintain standards and allowed his workcenter rating to decrease from Excellent to Satisfactory

o perception of favoritism affected morale and discipline within the section

o demonstrated lack of initiative and managerial skills, failed to maintain section equipment to standards o lacks enthusiasm in his duties and has no pride in his performance

o failed to develop subordinates; did not perform mandatory NCO-ER performance counseling

o failed to consistently inspect soldiers and their equipment, decreased unit readiness

o mediocre staff skills contributed to mediocre results during inspection

o fails to understand the importance of his position, avoids responsibility when possible

o avoids responsibility and is a negative influence on his section

o occasional challenge of authority affects his leadership ability with Soldiers

o demonstrates outstanding leadership and management skills but should work on staff skills

o failed to control section; allowed divisions to grow between group, fractured unity of effort

o allowed inappropriate behavior to continue until section became uncontrollable and discipline appeared arbitrary and ineffective

o needs to avoid the appearance of favoritism in order to restore squad morale

o fraternization with lower ranks and the appearance of favoritism is unacceptable and incompatible with effective leadership

o performance as NCOIC does not meet standards; recommend review of AR 600-100 o must understand the importance of enforcing standards and avoiding the appearance of favoritism or taking advantage of position

o inappropriate use of resources and abuse of authority; further abuses will result in relief of duties

o must improve management and discipline of troops to maintain order

o effective leaders lead by example; demonstrate your interest and support by participating in tasks

o need to improve work climate; sexual innuendo is harassment and is inappropriate and against regulations

o scheduling leaves needs improvement; cannot meet mission requirements when don't have sufficient people to do the job

o need to increase guidance of subordinates in their work

o supervision of subordinates needs improvement

o learn to trust subordinates and delegate; no one can do everything by themselves

o discipline troops when they need it; share concerns with NCOIC, refer discipline problems to Commander

o work ethic is outstanding but need to learn to share responsibility with subordinates; delegate effectively

o set clear and equal expectations for all subordinates to avoid perception of unequal treatment

o focus on correcting objectionable or inappropriate behavior on the spot rather than later to avoid appearance of acceptance

Training

Training is the teaching of skills and knowledge and the preparation, advancement, and qualification of individuals and units for duty performance. Effective training inevitably results in competence and good morale and discipline. Training should focus on wartime missions and address all responsibilities. The goal of training is sharing experience through informal instruction, learning from mistakes, and continuous professional growth.

o a consummate trainer; always mission-oriented

o able to properly counsel his subordinates on their progress

o academic average of 4 classes during the rated period was 95% with zero failures; a direct reflection on his ability

o achieved a 15% improvement in CTT scores through effective training and regular follow-up

o aggressive and innovative training methods ensured female weight lifting team placed 1st in Post tournament

o aggressively challenges Soldiers to perform to their potential; fosters professional growth

o all nine soldiers in his squad qualified expert on the M9 and M16A2; direct result of training, practice, supervision

o all 15 members of his section achieved a 1st time 100% pass on CTT; proven training skills

o all 5 of his mechanics earned the mechanics badge and completed over 50 hours of military correspondence courses

o all soldiers on his team qualified expert on assigned weapons; a rare result produced by relentless training o always ensured that all training schedules were accurately maintained and revised for maximum involvement

o always ensured that section training was regular, well planned, and professionally executed

o always prepared to provide training

o always willing to share his experience with others

o an excellent source of information for his fellow enlisted Soldiers ensuring they have the right information, follow the right procedures, and are properly prepared

o an experienced and vital part of the planning and execution of the company STX lane training

o arranged an instructional curriculum that improved the shop SQT scores an average of 20 points

o as a result of his support of the Education Program, many Soldiers in the unit are enrolling in continuing education classes

o as a result of his training and leadership, Battalion was lauded as "best ever" during AH-64 unit training

o as a result of his training, the HQ company surpassed four sister companies during Battalion weapons qualification

o as a result of his training, his Soldiers could readily assume the next higher duty position without hesitation

o as a tank Commander, scored a perfect score of 1,000 points on Tank Table VIII; teamwork and pride evident

o as Master Fitness Trainer, increased Soldier pass rate on APFT from 85 to 99 percent in less than a year

o as unit HAZMAT instructor, doubled the number of qualified handlers, improved safety

o assisted and motivated platoon to earn best in company for Drill and Ceremony 2 cycles in a row o assisted in development of a 75-lane land navigation course for state-wide use, increased training opportunities

o brigade CDR commended him for developing skill and self-confidence in Soldiers through martial arts training

o because of his training, not a single vehicle in the company has failed a road side inspection

o best Driver instructor in company; best results in Battalion

o best trainer in the company; always trusted with the most important classes

o built a winning attitude through tough and realistic training and a history of accomplishment

o certified 50 personnel throughout the Brigade on the EST 2000; dramatically improved quality of weapons training

o cited by the division Staff Judge Advocate office as having the best legal training program in the division

o coached 5 recruiters in all aspects of the recruiting profession; enlistment rates steadily climbing

o coached Soldiers to win both Battalion NCO and Soldier of the Quarter Boards

o coached the battalion's M60 machine gun team to a top placement in the CG's marksmanship competition

o coached the BN flag football team to win first place in the brigade tournament

o commended by Battalion Commander for implementing the first company-level PAI Program; improved reporting

o commended by BDE CDR for outstanding performance and dedication during Battalion gunnery exercise

o commended by the battalion commander for running the best training program within the battalion o completed a 48 hour Force Protection Academy including a hands-on C-IED lane; increased team effectiveness

o completed the Contracting Officer Representative Course

o complimented by the TRADOC IG team for maintaining a superior training program

o computerized training, operational, and administrative procedures; enhanced communication

o conducted NCODP classes for company on administrative and financial actions

o conducted multiple training events and staff assistance visits to increase standardization and compliance across the Brigade

o conducted numerous M16 ranges for the battalion; earned recognition for achieving 90 percent qualification rate

o conducted numerous small arms ranges qualifying over 1,000 soldiers

o conducted squad physical fitness program; delivered APFT average score of 270, best in company

o consistently briefed his soldiers before each training exercise to ensure maximum comprehension

o consistently worked to enhance and improve company training

o constantly commended on his instruction during Shared Training and Battle Lab FTX's

o constantly implemented new methods to improve his team's basic soldiering and signal communication skills

o continuously assisted students in subjects outside his own areas of expertise

o continuously set the standard for the company in all areas o created Command maintenance program standards and trained the IBP staff on PMCS and Unit Level Maintenance

o created the strongest staff section in the division by insisting on uncompromising standards of training

o created training plan based on the unit METL for the battalion NCO FTX; ensured 100% task coverage

o created a positive work environment by selflessly sharing knowledge and skills with seniors, peers, and subordinates

o cross-trained personnel on critical tasks; multiplied combat effectiveness

o dedicated and well organized trainer

o delegated effectively and supervised progress; developed well qualified leaders

o demanding and tough leader who communicates effectively

o demanded regular and consistent training; produced 100% qualification for entire platoon on all assigned weapons

o demonstrated a professionalism which inspired and encouraged Initial Entry soldiers

o demonstrated the patience and ability to clearly explain complex topics; improved Soldiers' understanding

o demonstrated the ability to encourage the best efforts of her team

o deployed on first aircraft to Desert Shield; provided in-depth NBC and battle field training upon arrival

o designed a professional development guide for Soldiers; currently in use army wide

o designed and implemented a company Soldier Handbook which greatly improved the company's success at NTC o despite no formal training, instructed peers and superiors on M1151; was solely responsible for training success

o developed a training budget of $55,000 to support all scheduled training demands for MTMC Europe

o developed a training plan that addressed the unit METL shortcomings; unit recognized as best in Battalion

o developed and implemented a special PT program which immediately produced results

o developed, implemented an intensive hands-on evaluation for MOS certification; overcame learning obstacles

o developed and initiated the IBP Brigade's first driver's training and dispatch program; qualified over 500 personnel

o developed effective BNCOC FTX-STX; adapted as the core of all future Noncommissioned Officer Academy programs

o developed company-level NCO Professional Development Program; praised by the Battalion CSM

o developed his Soldiers into a lethal fighting force capable of performing a full spectrum of combat operations

o developed junior NCOs by assigning them additional areas of responsibility

o developed training folders for all critical equipment items

o developed training plans for all NBC teams within the company; enforced 100% qualification

o developed training materials that enhance the soldiers' performance and duty related skills

o devised a Mission Essential Tasks List for the Post IG staff; dramatically increased productivity

o devised a training program that raised tank crew scores on TT VII by 50 pts o devoted his total attention, time, and effort to Soldier development

o directly responsible for Platoon receiving Brigade Commander's streamer for training excellence

o directly contributed to AIT company score of 98% on end of course APFT

o doubled the ANCOC training capacity to support the surge in SFC promotions

o due to his marksmanship background, was selected to train unit on M4 and M9 weapons firing

o during off-duty time rewrote or created all SOP's for the platoon; earned commendable rating during inspection

o dynamic teaching skills; motivated Soldiers to excel in their profession

o eager to share knowledge and experience; key to his section's 100% operational readiness

o earned 1st place overall for Battalion M4 shoot-out

o earned the Expert Infantryman's Badge

o effectively ensured training standards were met

o effectively rescheduled hundreds of Soldiers for make-up training with outstanding results

o emphasis on personal training resulted in 8 of 10 Drill Sergeants scoring above 90 on SQT

o emphasis on training and attention to detail produced a 100% pass rate for the EFMB; five soldiers earned badge

o encouraged a positive training environment by promoting teamwork

o energized training program to combat a critical shortage of drivers within Bn; reduced shortage, increased readiness o enforced a positive training environment

o enrolled every soldier in his platoon in the CLEP Program to earn college credit

o ensured 100% of directorate passed CTT

o ensured all of her Soldiers successfully completed PLDC and other career enhancing courses

o ensured Soldiers and NCOs understood training objectives

o ensured Soldiers were properly trained and prepared for war

o ensured that Soldiers were held to the highest standards for CTT and mandatory training

o ensured training was effective and timely

o ensured Soldiers are qualified on all assigned weapons and crew-served weapons; best qualification rate in Bn

o ensured soldiers are confident in primary MOS and cross-trained in next position

o ensured soldiers are competently trained on CTT

o enthusiastic, motivated, and dedicated to providing every Soldier with quality training

o established a 92Y training plan that greatly increased job performance and morale of team

o established a BDE drill team; resulted in 2 of his NCOs being accepted to all Army Drill Team

o established a comprehensive NBC defense plan during operation Desert Shield; imparted confidence to workcenter

o established a training program within the squad which decreased NMC vehicles by 40% and increased subordinate knowledge o established a Platoon NCOPD program that became the Company standard

o established common task training program that resulted in 100% first time go on CTT

o exceeded both the Georgia and the Army National Guard Bureau ship rate standard of 80% for training year 2010

o exceeding the Battalion standard, he trained three Soldiers to achieve an average score of 276

o excelled in Tank Table VIII gunnery training; his platoon achieved a 93% first time Go rate; best in the Brigade

o excellent hands-on trainer

o executed MOB training requirements culminating in 100% trained status

o exemplary performance as a trainer

o experienced trainer; excellent with individuals or groups

o expert knowledge and insight were vital during critical field training exercises

o expert training method ensured his Ranger Challenge Team placed in BDE Ranger Shootout; 1st win for the unit

o expert training methodology resulted in his section being the only one in the Bn to achieve a perfect score at Gunnery

o expertly coached 5 soldiers during and after duty hours to earn the EFMB

o expressed a positive learning attitude; was not intimidated by any task or working conditions

o extremely adept at preparing his section for professional and technical advancement

o flawlessly coordinated training and make-up training

o focused on mission-oriented training

o focuses on training IET students who require extra training

o generates positive attitude and enthusiasm in students

o gives constructive criticism to subordinates

o had no equipment down time in past 9 months due to improved maintenance qualification process

o hand-picked as the subject matter expert by BDE CDR to train all staff elements on TOC operations

o hand-picked by scuba team OIC to train 1st Group pre-scuba course

o has an extensive knowledge base from previous deployments and does not hesitate to share lessons learned

o has raised individual training proficiency from less than 50% to over 90%

o has guided Ranger Challenge Team to a history making first place finish in Brigade Ranger Shoot Out

o helped train the unit on the new SINCGARS radio system

o her K-9 section placed first overall in a 24-team competition

o her skills, knowledge, and experience make her a quality leader

o his Bn NCO certification program was recommended by USAREUR IG as the standard for Europe

o his company was recognized by CSA as the Army's best electronic warfare unit; direct result of his training ability

o his efforts directly contributed to the highest ever platoon APFT average in Battalion

o his counseling and training resulted in a 100% graduation rate for 25 students o his detachment achieved a 96% expert qual rate as a result of his marksmanship training program

o his drill and ceremony training resulted in his platoon being selected best in the company drill 2 cycles in a row

o his effective training techniques achieved a 15% increase in CTT scores; recognized by unit leadership

o his experience in TOC operations resulted in the only TOC operated solely by NCOs during a 9 month deployment

o his facilities were awarded TRADOC's Best Classroom Facilities honor

o his leadership resulted in a highly trained and motivated team during CMTC rotation

o his mentorship produced 1 BDE Soldier of the Quarter and 2nd runner-up for 2 quarters

o his no-nonsense approach to training contributed to his section being selected as the best 60mm crew in Bn

o his platoon exceeded all Brigade standards during NTC rotation

o his platoon received a 98% first-time pass rate in weapons qual as a result of his exceptional training

o his platoon recognized as major factor in the successful defense of the unit's perimeter during NTC, repelling three OPFOR attacks

o his section has been requested numerous times by the Signal Center for communication tests

o his sincere concern for Soldiers and meticulous training style turned 2 marginal soldiers into exceptional Soldiers

o his squad placed 1st of 9 and went on to represent unit in the Infantry Skills Competition; placed 2nd of 30 o his squads finished 1st and 2nd out of 20 squads in company "Top Gun" Competition

o his strong work ethic and detailed training plan produced a 25% increase in EIB recipients within the Battalion

o his team achieved 100% GOs during Battalion CTT

o his team received certificate of achievement for outstanding switch testing support from C-E Board

o his training motivated his unit to earn the Distinguished Marching Unit designation for excellence in D&C

o his training of the section contributed to the company 60mm mortar section being selected as best in the Bn

o his training produced competent, tough, and aggressive small-unit leaders

o identified specific warrior task training and leadership development skills essential for unit competency and exhibited exceptional proficiency in delivering them

o implemented continuous crew-served weapons training, improved number of combat-qualified soldiers from 7 to 20

o implemented environmental science training program; entire staff nationally recognized in food service certification

o improved his soldiers' SQT scores by 10 points

o improved PAC operations by 10% as a result of his training plan and mentorship of soldiers

o improved staff PT scores by 35 points by developing an intense PT program

o improved the skills and developed natural talent of subordinates

o incorporated tactical knowledge gained from three prior OEF deployments to prepare Soldiers for pending mission o increased the units ASI L4 qualification from 25% to 50% while assigned as the Operations NCO/Training NCO; key to the unit's improved readiness level

o initiated procurement of high tech communications van to aid in broadening team's skills

o inspired teamwork and a winning, professional attitude

o instilled the desire to put forth the maximum effort; motivated his NCOs to take on tough missions and win

o instituted MOS training for soldiers working outside their primary duties; erased previous inspection discrepancies

o instructed an indigenous force of 120 individuals in Spanish; increased communication, unified effort

o instructed foreign national students in their native language; received accolades from students/staff

o instrumental in training civilians on doctrine; resulted in a smooth fielding of battlefield software and interim hardware

o instrumental in training/coaching Battalion marksmanship team to win Post championship

o intense focus on maintenance training resulted in zero company vehicles failing a roadside inspection

o kept his Sergeants informed of changes to training and policies governing the conduct of training

o knowledge of supply operations ensured the unit won Division Quarterly Supply Award

o launched many successful careers with solid foundation

o licensed 12 soldiers within 30 days by developing and implementing a driver training program

o made commandant's list for the Movement Control Specialist Course o made well informed decisions; provided his Soldiers with an environment conducive to effective training

o magnificent training has resulted in 5 DA Culinary Arts Competition finalists

o maintained the team's weapons proficiency with ranges while deployed; personally coached additional close quarters marksmanship

o marksmanship instruction resulted in 96% of the detachment firing expert with the M16A2

o mentored 5 soldiers to achieve a perfect score on promotion board; coined by Battalion CSM

o mentored Regimental instructors to achieve an unprecedented 90% pass rate for the Ranger Course

o mentored two drill sergeants to be selected as Battalion Drill Sergeant of the Quarter

o meticulous attention to detail brought outstanding results for training areas

o meticulous training ensured Battalion M240B machine gun crews won 1st place in CG's marksmanship competition

o meticulous training resulted in 50 medical MOS students passing the National Certification Exam; 100% pass rate

o mission focused; received Army Achievement Medal for improvements made to METL

o motivated his entire squad to enroll in college, 3 graduate this fall

o motivated soldiers to learn due to his enthusiasm and broad knowledge of training subjects

o motivated trainer and mentor; personally prepared and trained his soldiers for Soldier, NCO, and promotion boards o motivated trainer who sets high standards; trained soldiers until standards were met; no soldier left behind!

o not intimidated by any task or working conditions

o obtained a 100% GO rating in Special Forces comm training

o on his own initiative, developed an Audie Murphy study tape; resulted in 10 soldiers being inducted

o orchestrated and developed training plan for 2 FTXs; completely NCO-led

o organized, trained, and led an OPFOR team which aggressed SOBC students participating in FTXs

o organized and ran four Tactical Site Exploitation training events; critiques were above average

o outstanding ability to instruct in accordance with TRADOC standards; time always used effectively

o outstanding teacher and coach

o patiently instructed CPR students until they understood and qualified for certification

o patiently rehearsed slower students until they fully understood each task

o perfect training record - 100% of soldiers trained passed all tests

o performed extremely well during three month long MSE New Equipment Training Crew Drills

o personal supervision ensured training effectiveness

o personally trained Division NCO of the Year after duty hours

o personally trained his soldiers for ARTEP, CTT, and SQT tasks; all 15 Soldiers met standards o pivotal during the unit pre-deployment CTT training, instructed 10 tasks at company level

o planned and executed combat training; prepared his platoon for the rigors of combat

o planned and executed exercise which successfully tested unit's deployment plan

o planned and executed the 1st BDE Military Stakes Competition; recognized by Division CSM for his work

o planned and organized an effective EFMB program in which 70% of the candidates received the badge

o planned, coordinated, and executed 1st NCO-run Battalion Live Fire Howitzer Section Evaluation

o planned and implemented a diet and nutrition program for overweight Soldiers; diet and conditioning increased scores

o platoon's training success key to earning four of five training streamers

o possesses strong technical and operational knowledge utilized by subordinates for personal growth

o prepared doctrinal training that will lead the NCO Corps into the next century

o primary trainer on the New RMC Mux/Demux Systems for much improved secure voice communications

o proactive approach to training increased quota utilization and reduced attrition by 35% for MOS 89D

o proactive in training his squad; always seeks training opportunities during down time

o proficient trainer; constantly teaches soldiers

o provided escalation of force, positive identification of targets, and ROE training for all Soldiers o provided extensive training on the M16A1 rifle to company Soldiers in preparation for CTT

o provided primary training to battalion medics which earned the section the Division EFMB Streamer

o provided the latest in course material by devoting after-duty hours to revising lesson plans

o quality performance as an Recruitment Sustainment Program trainer

o qualified 50 out of 50 with assigned weapons

o qualified expert on assigned weapon

o qualified superior on Bradley Table VIII

o quickly identified and developed plan to overcome training shortcomings

o received a Coin of Excellence from the Bde Cdr for conducting an outstanding Special Forces range in preparation for their upcoming Afghanistan rotation

o received accolades for his realistic and challenging training of reservists scheduled to deploy into combat

o received Armor School's Outstanding Instructor Award for demonstrated Excellence in tactical skills

o received commendable comments on numerous tests and training displays for MSE

o received commendable rating during an evaluation of Sergeants' Time training by the I Corps IG office

o received commendable rating in training during Brigade Inspection

o received outstanding critiques for his instructional expertise o recognized by Battalion Commander for excellence during Expert Field Medic Badge training

o recognized by MACOM CG for best training during Aerial Gunnery Exercise

o recognized for dramatically improving technical training by developing an MOS certification program in the Bn

o relieved a critical shortage of drivers within the unit through intensive classroom training and road testing

o rescued a sub-standard weight control program, increased unit APFT scores

o researched, designed, and executed highly realistic cavalry scout combat training program at the NTC

o revised and refined training strategies which enhanced the quality of squad level training

o rewrote, edited, and condensed a 600 page TACSOP into a user friendly document in 2 months

o saved the army $6,500 annually by developing a student handout that reduced POI man-hours by 60 hours

o selected above his peers for a TDY to New York to train West Point Cadets

o selected by the J3 and JTF CDR to train staff on all aspects of TOC operations

o selected twice during this rating period as Instructor of the Cycle; competed against 10 other instructors

o served as foreign weapons range NCOIC, qualified over 100 IBP soldiers in BRM, Short Range, and Close Quarters Marksmanship

o served as the Division's trainer on all aspects of wartime strength accounting; increased speed and efficiency o set high standards of personal performance and excels as a team player

o set the highest standards of technical competence in training

o Sergeant's Time Training was selected as the centerpiece for USAREUR Today television series

o shared knowledge and experience which was valued by junior officers and NCOs alike

o shared his knowledge and expertise with his team

o shared knowledge of operations and administration; enhanced performance of subordinates

o singled out by the Battalion CDR as having the best enlisted training program within the Battalion

o singled out as the driving force in winning TRADOC CDR's Award for Excellence for an Outdoor Training Facility

o singled out for his superior training program by the TRADOC IG

o spearheaded Convoy Protection Platform training development; course adopted by company for training incoming units to theater

o spent considerable time and effort passing his vast experience on to others

o spent numerous hours training team on problem areas; brought cell up to standards

o stressed safety first during all training events

o strives for maximum team performance

o successfully completed training with superior results

o successfully improved 5 units in all common task areas during Annual Training o supervised Pre-Marksmanship Instruction utilizing the EST- 2000 for the entire Brigade and numerous external units; a rare skill

o supervised training instructor rehearsals; ensured all instruction was logical and appropriate for Iraqi students

o tactical and technical proficiency exceeded that of his peers; excellent, results-oriented trainer

o takes pride in military knowledge and is eager to train others

o taught doctrine to civilians who successfully fielded hardware and interim software

o taught five common tasks to 98 soldiers; produced 100 percent go on annual CTT

o taught soldier skills and mentorship by using Battalion CIP as a positive teaching tool

o taught unit NCO Certification Program for newly assigned sergeants

o team player who trains students to achieve their maximum potential

o team player; assisted other platoons in accomplishing their mission and training objectives

o thorough in resourcing and delivery of training objectives

o trained 150 Iraq Army Soldiers on land navigation, reflexive fire, entering and clearing a room, and AK-47 weapons proficiency

o trained 50 Soldiers in the platoon on RETRANS operations and proper use of the ANCD in support of combat operations

o trained five tank companies for qualification gunnery with a 95% pass rate o trained 5 reserve component instructors in the train-the-trainer concept

o trained all medics in his section to proficiency; resulted in section winning Best Medic Section in Div streamer

o trained and conditioned six soldiers who failed the APFT to pass within four weeks

o trained and mentored junior leaders to create strongest staff section in the division

o trained battalion and brigade reenlistment NCOs to win 1st Qtr FY91 Reenlistment Award

o trained Forces Command Explosive Ordnance Disposal Team of the Year

o trained her NBC Teams to win four consecutive quarterly Battalion NBC Competitions

o trained her platoon in Night Land Navigation Course; result 100% first time go

o trained his crew on tank gunnery skills, HMMWV gunnery, dismounted operations, live fire shoot house, and air insertion techniques

o trained his OPFOR to receive a rating of Excellence; only one in the Battalion to receive this recognition

o trained his team to achieve assigned signal tasks

o trained over 50 officers from the former Soviet Republic of Moldova; received by name commendation

o trained platoon to achieve 100% first time go rate on M16 and hand grenade qualification

o trained platoon to consistently exceed 90% first time go rate in all training related areas

o trained platoon to maintain technical and tactical proficiency o trained soldiers to assume next higher position at any time

o trained soldiers to function as a cohesive, highly functional team

o trained staff to provide medical threat briefings to soldiers deploying to 13 different countries; coined by CG

o trained students to exceed normal standards

o trained the crew which won the 32d AADCOM Best Crew competition by scoring a perfect 1113 points

o training led subordinate to be top recruiter in company 7 out of 8 months

o training management excellence; students were always well informed and prepared for training

o trains for readiness and prepares for the unexpected

o trains for team competency

o trains his section to completely accomplish any and all tasks assigned

o trains subordinates to lead

o tutored 12 soldiers after duty hours; improved GT scores from an average of 99 to 115

o unit Training NCO; obtained 27 school slots for soldiers; to date, no one lacks military education

o unmatched capacity for training soldiers

o used battalion command inspection as a forum to teach soldier skills and improve NBC operations

o uses experience as a training tool

o uses unscheduled down time to train his soldiers on critical tasks o utilized his experience gained from previous deployments to clearly communicate and emphasize important concepts during IED Defeat lanes

o volunteered off-duty time to help train JROTC and ROTC students

o volunteered to teach Land Navigation to 120 students at the local high school JROTC class

o willingly shares his knowledge and insight

o willingly shares his vast knowledge and expertise with others

o willingly shares what he learns with lower enlisted soldiers

o willingly helps her peers; understands the need for teamwork

o won 32d AADCOM best crew competition; obtaining a perfect score of 1,000 points

o won Outstanding Instructor Award for demonstrated Excellence in tactical and technical skills

Needs Improvement (Training)

o does not use his free time to improve his knowledge of his MOS or to become a more efficient or better Soldier

o needs to devote more time to improving her knowledge and skills

o overcame several obstacles to advancement but requires further training before...

o increase training in order to meet all qualification requirements

o has made significant progress in qualification and may be ready for advancement

o demonstrated dedication and sincere effort to improve but limited by...

o performance is limited due to inability to qualify in...

o negatively affected our state of readiness by...

o failed to take advantage of opportunities to advance

o achieved full qualification in position and now needs to concentrate on...

o counseled by the Battalion CSM for having the least qualified platoon in the company

o failure to plan ahead or manage current training requirements reduced readiness

o his performance was below average and is in immediate need of retraining

o has limited patience, loses control when training

o is indifferent to suggestions for advancement and misses many opportunities for improvement o despite encouragement and efforts of peers, cannot qualify for duty and fails to make effort to improve

o will not use off-duty time for study or self-improvement, fails to advance in qualification

o failed to acquire the necessary skills and attributes to...

o needs to increase efforts to share experience and knowledge

o make effort to share knowledge and experience with all members of platoon to avoid appearance of favoritism

o unable to relate to trainee, does not possess good people skills

o despite the best efforts of trainers on and off-duty, was unsuccessful in...

o demonstrated a lack of knowledge in most assigned duties, does not comply with instructions and is a threat to the safety of this battery

o failed to formally document SOP, section unable to use or complete maintenance of newly fielded equipment

o ignored responsibility to develop documentation or train section on upgraded PRC-1077 radios, now secure comm is limited

o avoided sharing information on arrangements with peers until an unplanned TDY reduced present qualification rate to zero

Responsibility & Accountability

Responsibility is the proper care, use, and conservation of personnel, equipment, supplies, property, and funds. Maintenance of weapons, vehicles, equipment, and conservation of supplies and money is a special leadership responsibility because of its role in the success of all missions. It includes inspecting equipment often, holding Soldiers responsible for repairs and losses due to negligence, learning how to use and maintain all assigned equipment, and knowing the readiness status of weapons, vehicles, and other equipment at all times. It includes knowing where each Soldier is during duty hours, where they live, and their family or emotional condition. It involves reducing accidental manpower and monetary losses by providing a safe environment; it includes creating a climate that encourages young Soldiers to learn and grow and to report serious problems without fear of repercussions. In addition, responsibility means Soldiers, whether in charge or following orders, must accept responsibility for their actions.

o a serious leader who ensures all property is properly accounted for at all times

o a serious Soldier who uses garrison time to consider and counter all possible obstacles to mission

o a responsible, reliable Soldier who performs the tedious, behind-the-scenes work without reward or expectation of recognition

o accomplished the closeout of all Class, I, II, and IX accounts, and the turn in of the facilities in Kuwait; boosted supply availability o an OL Chief with integrity who demonstrated effective stewardship by example, left joint facilities in better condition than when he arrived

o accepts responsibility for his actions and the results of his Soldiers' actions

o accepts responsibility not only for himself but for his subordinates as well

o acted with the highest level of discipline and dedication to the mission through diligent maintenance; 98% operational readiness rate

o actively encourages off-duty education and professional growth in subordinates; increased section skills

o always concerned with safety; no incidents or injuries since her arrival

o always maintains issued and squad equipment in a high state of readiness

o always performs daily inventories and generator checks

o arranged free FCC license preparatory class for Soldiers resulting in all receiving licenses

o brought the company into compliance with all OSHA, HAZMAT and safety regulations and reduced safety incidents by 50%

o can always be counted on to conduct daily checks and safe inventories

o can be trusted to carry out instructions; dependable

o careful analysis of expenditures identified inconsistent and unsatisfactory compliance with contract requirements, improved maintenance support

o chose the hard right over the easy wrong; demanded that his Soldiers did the same o committed to effective management of personnel and resources

o completes assigned and daily shift duties without supervision, can be counted on when all others fail

o completed over 100 combat missions and logged over 2K miles with no accidents or injuries

o conceived and developed database procedures that improved tracking that were adopted by the entire Brigade

o conducted all quality assurance inspections of Air Mobile equipment prior to deployment; ensured readiness

o conscientious and efficient, the only mechanic who still has a full set of tools

o conscientious and deliberate actions and attention to detail helped ensure accurate accountability

o consistently accomplished more in less time with fewer Soldiers and resources

o constantly improved maintenance practices and procedures; ensured optimum mission readiness

o consistently maintained his training aids to standards between AIT classes; only instructor with current support material

o constantly seeks and accepts additional responsibilities

o continued to complete his duties as Platoon Sergeant while holding the position of Acting First Sergeant

o continues to seek and accept responsibility

o controlled all of the Battalion's life fire exercises for over 5,000 155mm artillery rounds with no firing incidents

o cooperated with sister components to the benefit of all concerned to produce most accurate activity reports to date o coordinated the chassis re-alignment of over 100 vehicles and military equipment; facilitated better performance

o created a climate in which soldiers were encouraged to learn and advance their qualifications

o created a climate that encouraged soldiers to excel and meet every challenge

o created reporting procedures for the IBP's assigned vehicles and equipment; standardized NMC reporting

o dedicated, hard working individual who demonstrated his responsibility through the maintenance and condition of his assigned equipment

o delegated tasks effectively to subordinates; shared responsibility and credit for success

o delivered support on time and on target

o demanded that security was maintained during all operations even in familiar surroundings; protected crew

o demands high standards for maintenance and control of military property; enjoys best uptime rate in Brigade

o demonstrated selfless service and desire to accomplish the mission; facilitated a seamless transition and successful draw down in Iraq

o dependable; only Soldier in unit that can always be relied on to have up-to-date TMs and deployment-ready inventory

o diligent and tireless, managed over $2 million in inventory across seven FOBs with zero losses on redeployment

o demonstrated outstanding organizational abilities; ensured the maintenance and upkeep of 10 wheeled vehicles and trailers with a property book value of over $1.5 million

o does what is right always, an example to his peers

o drove over 5,000 miles in a combat environment without a safety related incident or damage to equipment

o earned a commendable rating for key control during Brigade command inspection

o effective oversight of complex arrangement of support delivered best recovery rate ever experienced, CONUS or abroad

o efficiently managed a budget in excess of $300,000

o emphasized risk management and safety and reduced safety incidents; resulted in no loss of life, limb, or eyesight during combat tour

o encouraged career progression which resulted in all assigned soldiers enrolling in continued education

o encouraged his Soldiers to continue formal education to improve their future opportunities, resulted in 100% enrolled in college courses

o encouraged squad members to enroll in Army correspondence courses

o encouraged subordinates to continue their formal education for advancement; three squad members enrolled

o encourages the best from his Soldiers; all his Soldiers enrolled in courses for higher education

o enforced high safety standards during Combat Logistics Patrols, over 30,000 accident-free miles in a combat environment

o enforced strict field training exercise procedures to ensure safety and no loss of time for soldiers

o ensured assigned equipment is always serviceable and maintained for mission readiness o ensured that load plans were properly developed and adhered to; no loss of sensitive items or equipment due to negligence

o ensured all equipment was on hand and serviceable

o established and maintained high standards for barracks maintenance

o exercised responsibility for daily maintenance and accountability of facilities and equipment

o follows orders and standing guidance even when other Soldiers ignore it

o gained 100% accountability within 30 days of assuming position vacated by an NCO relieved for fraud, waste, and abuse

o hard working, dedicated NCO; demonstrated by his daily actions, the meaning of integrity

o helps soldiers develop skills through timely advice, guidance, and planning

o her initiative to conduct a complete inventory of the radio warehouse, found and added over 300 unaccounted-for radio sets worth $5 million to CORE IMS for future issue

o his diligence ensured 100% accountability of section and company communications equipment

o his emphasis on driver safety resulted in 600,000 miles of accident-free vehicle operation for his platoon

o his emphasis on safety resulted in 365 accident-free days

o his emphasis on safety resulted in his squad members being awarded the Drivers Badge

o his platoon maintained accident free year despite continuous rotation and changing mission o his safety program and enforcement resulted in accident-free training

o his section earned praise from several units across the battalion AOR for the high level of support it provided to organic and tenant units

o implemented Fabric and Canvas repair at DS level; produced tremendous budget savings for unit

o implemented policies which significantly reduced the number of injuries within his platoon

o implemented changes when necessary to improve unit operations and efficiency

o in the absence of guidance, always made sound and timely decisions

o initiated unit recycling program which reduced waste

o inspires and enforces growth and excellence; 55 percent of his platoon enrolled in college

o inspired growth and advancement in subordinates

o instilled safety consciousness, responsibility, and integrity in Soldiers

o inventoried and consolidated repair parts during movement from FOB Delta to COS KALSU resulting in minimal down time for the maintenance section

o inventoried, packed platoon's equipment appropriately in preparation for numerous training events and deployments ; no equipment lost a result of his attention to detail

o is willing to accept ultimate responsibility

o key to company receiving Brigade recognition for safety excellence o learned how to troubleshoot the AN/PRC-145 radio and load new keys with the SKL; assured critical convoy communications

o led the way; ensured all assigned vehicles were always mission ready

o made prudent and economical use of funds

o made risk assessment an integral part of training

o maintained 100% accountability of more than $1.5 million of equipment

o maintained a 100% operational readiness rating on his M1A2 battle tank and M1114 HMMWV during OIF 04-06

o maintained accountability and maintenance of over $6,000,000 worth of facilities and equipment

o maintained over 20 COMSEC accounts with 100% accountability and zero COMSEC Compromises or reportable COMSEC incidents

o maintained an accident-free 24 month period

o maintained team equipment and readiness

o maintained thorough accountability of unit's Class IX budget; eliminated waste

o managed resources in a highly efficient manner

o mature; has the ability to perform at a higher level of responsibility even without the support or presence of his supervisor

o mentored and motivated his Soldiers to continue their college education resulting in them completing 66 credit hours while deployed

o my most dependable technician; TMs always up to date, job log always empty o no loss of property during three training exercises and one NTC rotation; most effective management to date

o obtained equipment on own initiative and developed the first known standard within DOD for reclaiming used oil

o only Soldier in bn who, in absence of orders, took responsibility and scheduled equipment for maintenance; prevented mission failure

o our go-to man; can always be trusted to have the most reliable and functional equipment in battalion

o oversaw use of over $1.5 million worth of equipment, resulting in no loss or significant damage during combat operations

o personally responsible for unit's excellent safety record

o practiced conservation of supplies and funds which resulted in commendable supply inspections

o prevented waste by setting the example himself; reduced paper usage by half

o proactive; diligent planning identified several overlooked and neglected areas of coverage and facilitated their immediate improvement

o professional Soldier; can be relied on to have operational, deployment-ready equipment

o promoted safety consciousness and responsibility in Soldiers

o promoted Soldiers' professional development through innovative educational programs

o puts forth maximum effort; enjoys challenge, thrives on responsibility

o readily accepted responsibility for failure but recognizes success of subordinates o received commendable ratings for physical security during Brigade Command Inspection

o reliable Soldier who understands the importance of his duties and their key role in supporting entire Brigade's effort

o resisted exploiting position or status for personal gain

o responsible and accountable; a very dependable NCO

o sacrificed personal time to brief soldiers on career enhancement opportunities in today's Army

o sacrificed numerous hours of his personal time to ensure reports were accurate and to standards before submitting

o safety briefings resulted in zero training accidents; constantly encouraged subordinates to accept more responsibility

o safety-oriented during all phases of training; reduced risk to personnel during rehearsals

o saved the Army more than $100,000 a year by sustaining serviceability of various vehicle components

o set the example for subordinates by always following guidance

o shares responsibility and credit for mission success with subordinates

o signed for and maintained 100% accountability of $25 million worth of deployed equipment during OEF

o stable and trustworthy, as Sergeant, serves as the foundation of a battle-ready squad

o stands up for and does what is right

o stepped up to the plate in absence of element leader, accepted and performed leadership duties in a positive manner with exceptional results o stressed career development and competitive nature of military advancement to his Soldiers

o stressed safety first; trained with zero accidents

o strictly enforced all safety policies and regulations

o suffered no injuries within his squad during 2 NTC rotations, the result of continuous oversight

o supports peers and superiors by foresight, planning, and constructive criticism of unsupportable plans

o sustained 95 % operational readiness rate for platoon equipment despite lack of funding

o takes responsibility for good, bad, right, and wrong; makes no excuses

o took initiative and performed all of the vehicle maintenance duties in the absence of the company motor sergeant

o took responsibility for his actions in all circumstances; good example for subordinates

o took responsibility seriously; researched his duties and made sure all requirements complied with; most dependable Soldier in squad

o taught Soldiers the importance of individual responsibility which improved accountability of issued equipment

o the only Soldier I can count on to perform daily shift checks and safe inventories without being told

o the only Soldier in Bn with 100% complete and operational deployment kit; assigned to coach others

o thrifty with all expendable supplies, accomplishes mission with no reduction in effectiveness

o took a special interest in Soldiers' family issues

o trusted by CSM because of his history and reputation for thorough preparation and training

o understands serious consequences of failure to prepare and imparts that urgent knowledge to subordinates

o uses down time to research and prepare for possible eventualities; the most prepared Soldier in camp

o voluntarily contributed observations to help fellow AIT instructors achieve Senior Instructor status

o volunteered for, planned, and participated in an overweight PT program that resulted in our platoon losing a combined weight of over 70lbs

o willingly accepted extra duty of certified mail handler for FOB Salerno and FOB Lightning, solemnly executed responsibility

o wise, efficient, and prudent manager of scarce resources

o with little formal training, SPC Smith became First Platoon's subject matter expert and authority on three different communication systems

Needs Improvement (Responsibility)

o follows orders under supervision but does not attempt to be an independent problem solver

o works well under supervision but needs to develop self-discipline and work independently

o needs to realize importance of performing daily tasks and the effects of ignoring them

o is uncooperative when corrected and displays a consistent lack of interest in section goals

o should review safety regulations and seek guidance from experienced NCOs on range safety

o make effort now to improve performance and restart career; cannot be depended on now to deliver on time

o must focus on training and ensure daily review with supervisor in order to improve performance

o his failure to follow orders led to the loss of his security clearance and now section is undermanned and unable to meet quota

o cannot be depended on and is frequently late for shift; recommend...

o reported to work under the influence of alcohol and was unable to execute his duties as...

o was entrusted with our most critical and essential tasks but disappointed his supervisors by...

o cannot be relied upon to maintain production rate in the absence of supervision

o cannot be trusted to oversee safe delivery of cargo; must be supervised at all times o was and is negligent in meeting his responsibilities causing numerous obstacles to mission accomplishment

o failure to supervise subordinates or follow procedures resulted in the loss of $2,000 worth of equipment

o unexcused absence from duty left Soldiers unsupervised

o failed to understand the importance of his duties, takes advantage of every opportunity to avoid responsibility

o needs to improve performance; focus on the basics: arrive at work on time, participate in PT, spend free time reviewing OIs

o demonstrated little regard for the security and accountability of sensitive items during deployments

o needs to improve efforts to track high value assets and focus on details of job

o performance is not satisfactory; seek training and advice from supervisor to get career back on track

o need to reduce Soldiers' qualification failures by increasing study time; make time available for study

o increase efforts to maintain government facilities; unreported alarm outages are not acceptable and threaten security

o follow in-place guidance; do not hinder efforts of safety monitor

o had to be constantly reminded to counsel and mentor Soldiers on a regular basis

Senior Rater Comments

The senior rater is the senior rating official in the military rating chain. Senior raters use their position and experience to evaluate the rated Soldier from a broad organizational perspective based on their experience. Their validation of the evaluation is the link between the day-to-day observation of the rated Soldier and the longer term evaluation of the rated Soldier's potential based on consecutive evaluation reports.

o a complete leader; one of a kind at taking care of Soldiers

o a confident leader that is dedicated to ensuring his Soldiers are well trained

o a dynamic performer and multifunctional NCO who is sought out across the Command for his extraordinary leadership capabilities

o a first-rate non-commissioned officer who is willing to face up to any task and tackle the issues head on

o a positive, can-do attitude; an example to his peers and subordinates

o a rare mix of intelligence and initiative; consistently achieves excellent results across a broad range of responsibilities

o a real team player

o a strong leader with a wealth of experience and knowledge

o a true professional who's always in the middle of our most critical processes; promote immediately!

o a young NCO who is striving to become one of the best

o absolutely superior NCO; excelled in job performance, community service, and leadership; promote at once

o accepts nothing less than 100%

o adjusts quickly to new situations and accepts responsibility for her actions

o aggressive competitor; takes great pride in exceeding accomplishments of others

o aided Facility Management for 3 months; showed great efficiency and versatility

o always excels as a Soldier and a leader

o always mission-oriented; thorough analytical skills; articulate in written and spoken communications

o always succeeded in all situations and circumstances

o always took a no-nonsense approach and stated opinion in a straight forward manner

o an exceptional NCO and capable leader; performed duties as vehicle mechanic in an outstanding manner

o assign as a platoon sergeant now; his knowledge will enhance unit's ability to accomplish their mission

o assign this Sergeant to teach future leaders: West Point, ROTC, any NCO academy

o assign to challenging leadership positions

o assign to challenging positions which require the most of an NCO

o assumed additional workloads regardless of size or complexity

o attacked every mission with vigor and zeal

o bearing is beyond reproach

o best Drill Sergeant in Brigade

o can accomplish any mission

o can handle any position; held Platoon Sergeant and Section NCOIC position simultaneously with great success

o challenge this NCO with positions of greater responsibilities

o challenge with positions of greater authority

o clearly a superior Senior NCO with unlimited potential; will serve the Army well at the most senior levels of enlisted leadership

o clearly demonstrated potential for unlimited advancement

o committed NCO who lives by "mission first, Soldiers always"

o competent, confident, caring leader of the highest caliber

o confident and dependable, quickly becoming an integral member of the workcenter

o conscientious, dedicated, and responsible NCO

o consistently made independent decisions that have merit and logic

o consistently performed above standards; achieved outstanding results

o consistently performed two pay grades above contemporaries

o consummate professional; promote ahead of peers

o continue to place in tough, demanding leadership jobs

o daily performance routinely exceeded the highest professional standards o dedicated and enthusiastic NCO with unquestionable integrity

o dedicated Senior NCO; allegiance to mission inspires peers, made this NCO invaluable team member; promote

o dedicated to the mission

o dedication to mission is unequalled; remains unflappable and productive under stressful conditions

o demonstrated potential for continued excellent performance at a higher rank

o demonstrated the ability to perform at the next higher grade

o demonstrated the potential for higher degrees of responsibility

o demonstrated qualities of a more senior NCO

o demonstrated the capacity for increased responsibility at the platoon level

o demonstrated the confidence needed to face the Army's toughest challenges; promote

o demonstrated management skills found in more experienced NCOs

o dependable, motivated, and trustworthy; a Senior NCO with the courage to manage without visible support

o devoted to his responsibilities; admirable attitude

o discharged responsibilities with complete professionalism

o displayed constant loyalty to superiors and allegiance to mission

o displayed strengths of an exceptional leader

o displayed exceptional leadership qualities, ability to get the job done; recommend promotion/retention o displayed unlimited potential

o earned trust, loyalty, and support from everyone in the battalion

o easily the best platoon sergeant assigned; his platoon out-performed all others in the company

o enthusiastic NCO that should stay with soldiers

o epitomizes what every NCO should be: aggressive, intelligent, and professional

o exacting approach to work; pays attention to detail

o excelled in every assignment and tasking

o excellent technical abilities; consistently performs high quality work

o exceptional devotion to Army ethics and personal values

o exceptional enthusiasm demonstrated daily

o exceptionally talented NCO who leads by example and serves with extreme pride

o exceptionally well organized and perceptive; solves Soldier problems easily

o executed his responsibilities with pride and professionalism

o exhibits the ability to be an effective Division Corps CSM

o extremely conscientious and highly motivated to succeed

o extremely well organized and perceptive to the problems and needs of subordinates

o exudes self-confidence in all aspects of his work

o first rate professional; shows ability and initiative to assume greater responsibility; promote now

o flawless and consistent performance

o flexible and versatile leader with boundless potential, ready to assume 1SG responsibilities

o genuine concern and unselfish dedication to duty

o groom this Staff Sergeant for Command Sergeant Major

o hard charging Soldier whose willingness to advance has set him apart from his peers; promote!

o hard working, versatile NCO; quickly section qualified, challenge with more responsibilities

o has the potential to perform duties as platoon sergeant

o her merits earned selection for career-development training ahead of peers

o high level of motivation; instills esprit de corps in superiors and subordinates alike

o highly mature and reliable NCO

o highly motivated Senior NCO who is committed to accomplishing the mission and taking care of Soldiers; clearly a future Command Sergeant Major

o highly skilled and dedicated professional, performs far beyond expectations; outstanding asset to the unit

o highly skilled member and motivated NCO; valuable asset to the unit and vital to Army mission; promote!

o his integrity, bearing, and confidence are inspiring

o his knowledge base is superior; potential is unlimited

o his potential is unlimited

o his tactical proficiency and experience made him extremely reliable in all situations

o innovative NCO, not afraid to take risks to improve mission results o is relied upon to give well conceived, mature opinions and judgments

o is technically and tactically proficient

o key to the battalion's flawless redeployment to CONUS

o knowledgeable and conscientious

o leads by example

o leads from the front; outstanding NCO role model

o loyal, tactful, and modest leader

o maintains the highest personal and professional standards

o managed Soldiers' schedules and technical skill training resulting in 99% patrol reliability rate

o master of his trade; I rely on his knowledge and expertise on the system configuration; promote

o mature and confident Soldier with extraordinary knowledge and initiative; immediately promote to SFC!

o mature NCO who understands the need for order and discipline

o motivated and self-confident Soldier

o multi-talented and accomplished leader and Soldier

o my number one Mobility line troop, can always be counted on to ensure compliance with requirements

o outstanding individual performance; select for Command Sergeant Major

o outstanding leader and top performer, delivered stellar results during Global War on Terrorism

o outstanding NCO that is truly dedicated to the unit's mission o outstanding NCO who leads by example; a solid professional ready for increased responsibility; promote!

o outstanding NCO with crisp military bearing and appearance; exceeds standards in military courtesies, fitness, and job performance

o outstanding performer; promote now

o outstanding role model; sets the NCO standard

o outstanding Soldier with a can-do attitude; always ready for more challenging tasks with greater responsibility

o outstanding team player! Propelled unit to win 2009 "OL of the Year" award; promote immediately!

o performance as Acting Battalion CSM was excellent

o physically fit; in tremendous condition; will succeed

o possesses a strong and positive drive toward professional development of platoon

o possesses great amount of integrity, sound judgment, and professionalism

o possesses superior personnel and administrative skills

o possesses the leadership skills necessary to lead any company on the battlefield

o possesses unlimited potential; displays untiring desire for excellence

o potential is unlimited; outstanding leader, coach, and mentor

o professional and competent leader

o promote ahead of peers; a total Army asset

o promote and make First Sergeant now; he's ready to run his own company now o promote immediately and assign as a Special Forces company Sergeant Major

o promote immediately; send to First Sergeant course

o promote now and select for ANCOC

o promote now to Sergeant First Class ahead of peers

o promote now; will be an excellent combat engineer unit First Sergeant

o promote to Sergeant First Class immediately; his leadership is needed by Soldiers

o promoted harmony and teamwork, increased focus

o proved himself as battle-tested non-commissioned officer, quickly took charge in combat operations

o puts the Army, mission, and soldiers before her self

o recognized as the best supply sergeant in battalion

o resourceful, agile, and reliable NCO

o rock-solid performer; consistently provides high-caliber maintenance and technical direction

o select for advanced NCO schooling and assign to challenging duty positions

o select for ANCOC and promote immediately

o select for attendance to Sergeant Major Academy

o select for CSM now

o select for First Sergeant now; groom for Command Sergeant Major

o selected as top performer of the quarter for 3rd Quarter 2010; displayed leadership, professionalism

o self starter; limitless drive and initiative

o send to ANCOC immediately; promote ahead of peers

o send to BNCOC, assign to troop leadership positions

o set and achieved high personal standards

o should be given increased responsibility as food service sergeant of a major subordinate command

o Soldier-oriented NCO

o stands up for what is right

o strongly motivated to succeed

o superior leader and professional; sets a high standard for his peers to emulate; ready for promotion

o superior performer in every respect; a strong leader

o taking care of Soldiers and superiors is his number one priority

o technically and tactically proficient; discharges duties with complete professionalism

o this NCO needs no supervision

o this Sergeant has a vast amount of knowledge

o tireless in the pursuit of mission success

o to maximize his potential, assign to positions of increased responsibility

o top notch technical abilities key to mission support, ready for increased supervisory responsibility; promote!

o total Army asset; select for First Sergeant now

o totally dedicated to excellence

o trains for readiness and the unexpected

o trained his subordinates to succeed

o turned his failing platoon around in 3 short months

o unequaled service to unit

o unique and rare talent; promote now ahead of peers

o unlimited potential for positions of increased responsibility

o unlimited ability; will succeed in the toughest jobs

o unlimited talent and drive; assign to challenging positions

o unlimited enthusiasm; continue to assign to positions of increased responsibility

o utilized common sense and courtesy while performing duties in a professional manner

o very tactful in dealing with seniors

o watch this Sergeant's career closely; he has a lot of potential

o well organized and versed in investigative techniques

o will excel in higher positions

o will make an outstanding First Sergeant

o willing to learn and grow

o works best with mission orders

Needs Improvement (Senior Rater Comments)

o unable to report to work on time and needs constant supervision; retention is not advised

o frequently late for work, sets a poor example for subordinates

o SSG Smith is uncooperative with leadership

o needs to realize cooperation is necessary and improve relationship with supervisor and chain of command

o fails to understand the difference between "taking care of troops" and following orders

o must accept responsibility for leadership and support HHQ decisions

o combative attitude is counter-productive and a liability to this Command

o performance has been affected by personal conflict and must be resolved in order for section to reach goals

o requires constant supervision, is unreliable, and should be relieved of duty

o resists suggestions for improvement and actively works against the orders of his superiors

o put forward much effort but unable to progress; consider reclassification

o not fit for this type of activity, exhibits a negative attitude and should be disqualified

o has the potential to be an excellent technician but is often careless with...

o cannot work with peers and is counter-productive

o does not possess the qualities necessary to advance to the next level

o allowed the pressure of family issues to affect her performance

o recommend release from duties and counseling until such time she can resume work without endangering others

o lacks maturity, displays poor judgment, needs further development

o despite increasing assistance and training, continues to have difficulty completing assigned tasks; recommend reclassification

o recommend immediate financial and psychological counseling for gambling problem

o lacks experience and fails to understand the importance of advancement

o unable to adjust to deployment or the diverse demands of a joint environment

o encouraged abuse of the system by using sick days as time off

o needs to realize importance of completing assigned tasks

o probably the worst performer in our Command

o is difficult for others to work with

o good performer with potential to be an outstanding Soldier and a valuable asset

o demonstrated a lack of skill in some duties, has potential, should double training efforts o does not comply with regulations and is a threat to the safety of this battery; recommend discharge at earliest opportunity

o takes advantage of every opportunity to avoid duty

o demonstrated an immature pride in avoiding responsibility and work

o unable to perform even the most basic tasks without help

o should never be put in charge of Soldiers

o lacks initiative, has to be told to perform the most obvious and needed tasks

o abused trust by failing to complete assignments

o has unearned sense of entitlement; complains bitterly when scheduled for night shifts or deployment

o fails to use TM or take adequate care in duties; reckless

o exhibited immoral pride in padding medical records for future, planned VA medical claims; worst example of integrity for new recruits

Awards

Awards make up a significant portion of promotion points and their importance should not be underestimated. Medals often make the difference in being promoted or spending another year in the same pay grade.

If you haven't submitted someone for an award or service medal before it might seem difficult but it's not really that hard. The process for recommending someone for an award is simple and follows the procedure and format described in AR 600-8-22, Military Awards. This book doesn't attempt to list rules and requirements for awards. The requirements are generally well known although they may differ from unit to unit depending on leadership and circumstances.

There are two broad categories of awards: those awarded for meritorious service and those awarded for a specific achievement.

Meritorious service is characterized by exemplary service over a long period of time. Examples of awards for meritorious service are the Army Achievement Medal or Army Commendation Medal awarded when a Soldier completes a permanent change of station.

Achievement awards are awards earned by performing a specific act such as completing a significant project or rescuing a flood victim. This type of performance is also recognized with the award of the Army Achievement Medal or the Army Commendation Medal.

Definitions:

Narrative. The narrative is the text that justifies the approval of the recommended award. The required justification varies depending on the type of award. The lower the award, the less support is required. The only justification required for the Army Achievement Medal, the Army Commendation medal, and the Meritorious Service Medal is the completion of the four achievement blocks (block 20) on the DA Form 638. Higher awards require substantial justification which is submitted as a separate attachment. In the past, most awards required written justification and that justification was a story-like, chronological description of the recipient's performance. That description came to be known as the narrative because it narrated the acts of the award recipient. Note that the word, narrative, is also used as a term for the citation text.

Citation. The citation is the text that will be read during the presentation of the award and printed on the award certificate. The required length of the citation depends on the type of award. The lower the award, the less content is required (or allowed). The citation length for the Army Achievement Medal, the Army Commendation medal, and the Meritorious Service Medal is limited to the space provided in the last block of the DA Form 638 (6 lines). Citations for all other awards are limited to nine lines and may be submitted on letter size bond paper as an attachment.

Certificate. The certificate or award certificate is the formal official document presented to the recipient that lists the circumstances of the award (name, unit, date, and a narrative description of the act that resulted in the award). A different form, depicting the medal awarded, is used for each award.

Meritorious Achievement. Meritorious Achievement is an act which is well above the expected duty performance. The act should be an exceptional accomplishment with a definite beginning and ending date. The length of time is not a primary consideration; however, speed of accomplishment of an important task can be a factor in determining the value of an act. Examples of meritorious achievement are the completion of a significant project or the rescue of a stranded flood victim.

Meritorious Service. Meritorious service is distinguished by outstanding service over a sustained period of time. For service to be considered meritorious, an individual's performance must exceed that expected of his or her rank and experience and be based on performance during an entire tour of duty. Awards presented when a Soldier PCSs recognize meritorious service. Meritorious service is exemplary performance over an extended period of time.

References:

AR 600-8-22, Military Awards

AR 600-8-19, Enlisted Promotions and Reductions

AR 672-20, Incentive Awards

AR 600-8-105, Military Orders

AR 670-1, Wear and Appearance of Army Uniforms and Insignia

Award Submission Requirements

AWARD	ERB	DA FORM 638	SEPARATE NARRATIVE	EYEWITNESS STATEMENT	SEPARATE CITATION	SUPPORTING DOCUMENTATION	POINTS
Army Achievement Medal	×	×					15
Army Commendation Medal	×	×					20
ARCOM with V Device	×	×	×	×			20
Meritorious Service Medal	×	×					25
Bronze Star Medal	×	×	×		×		30
Bronze Star with V Device	×	×	×	×	×	×	30
Soldiers Medal	×	×	×	×	×		35
Legion of Merit	×	×	×		×		35

The Army Achievement Medal

The Army Achievement Medal is the most commonly presented award and is worth 15 promotion points.

To recommend someone for an Army Achievement Medal, all you have to do is fill out a DA Form 638. No separate citation, narrative, or other attachments are required.

The Army Achievement Medal is awarded to any member of the Armed Forces who distinguished himself or herself by meritorious service or achievement of a lesser degree than required for award of the Army Commendation Medal.

The support justifying award of the Achievement Medal should be in bullet format in the four blocks provided on the DA Form 638. The citation for the Army Achievement Medal is limited to six lines. Army policy does not restrict the use of abbreviations and acronyms in award citations. However, due to the historical value of awards and the acts or service they represent, it is important that its appearance is professional and dignified. It is also recommended that only the most common abbreviations and acronyms be used in the citation. The abbreviation or acronym should be spelled out the first time and followed by the abbreviation or acronym in parenthesis. Certificates should include a brief narrative but should not be so brief as to distract from its importance.

How to Complete the DA Form 638

The requirements for submitting someone for a medal, whether it's an Achievement Medal or a Bronze Star, are largely the same but there are some important differences. They all require submission of the DA Form 638 and for some medals, like the Army Achievement Medal and the Army Commendation Medal, that's all that's required. But for higher awards, like the Army Commendation Medal with V Device or Bronze Star, more support (accompanying paperwork) is required. To avoid confusion, these instructions will address only the Army Achievement Medal. The official reference for filling out the DA Form 638 is AR 600-8-22, Military Awards, Table 3-2.

Block 1. Fill in the office information of the next office above the recommender in the Chain of Command. This is the office with approval authority.

Block 2. Enter the recommender's office information.

Blocks 3-7. Self Explanatory

Block 8. Fill in the individual's previous awards. The Army Service Ribbon (ASR), Korean Defense Service Medal (KDSM), Kuwait Liberation Medal (KULIBM), and Southwest Asia Service Medal (SWASM) are *service* medals and should not be listed.

Block 9. Enter the Service and Component of the person being recommended. Use the following:

Services	Component
USA - Army	Act - Active Duty
USMC - Marine Corps	Res - Reserve Forces
USN - Navy	NG - National Guard
USAF - Air Force	

Block 10. Enter the award being recommended (AAM) and the number of previous awards/oak leaf cluster (if applicable).

Block 11-19. Self Explanatory

Block 20. Use the space provided in the DA Form 638 to fill in the Soldier's achievements or meritorious service using bullet format.

Block 21. Enter the citation (see examples on following pages).

Block 22. Staff Section Admin Clerk should sign and date verifying individual is eligible for the recommended award.

Block 23-25. Fill in intermediate commander's information as appropriate.

Block 26. Approval Authority

a. ORDERS ISSUING AUTHORITY

b. CDR, MNC-I APO AE 09999

e. JOHN Q. PUBLIC

f. COL

g. COMMANDING

Block 27. Orders Issuing Headquarters

a. HQ, MNC-I APO AE 09999

Block 28. Name of Orders Approval Authority

a. JOHN A. SMITH

b. MSG

c. Chief, CJ1 Personnel Actions

Block 29-30. Leave blank

Block 31. Distribution

1-SOLDIER
1-UNIT
1-FILE
1-OMPF

Award Bullet Examples

To be effective, bullets entered on the DA Form 638 should follow the same guidance as used for NCOER bullet statements. They should state exactly what was accomplished and the positive result or effect of that action. The bullet statements used in NCOERs during the period covered by the award are a good source of material.

AR 600-8-22, Military Awards, requires that the narrative description (the justification) of meritorious service or achievement for award of the Army Achievement Medal be limited to bullet format in the space allowed on the DA Form 638.

The DA Form 638 contains four separate blocks for listing individual accomplishments, each block being limited to four lines. Note that many of the examples provided in this book go beyond the simple bullet statement format required by the regulation.

Follow the guidance below when documenting performance in block 20 of the DA Form 638:

- Use numerals for numbers 10 and above and spell out numbers lower than 10 (two, nine, etc). The exception is if numbers lower than 10 are used in the same sentence as numbers greater than 10, use numerals for all numbers (1 truck, 9 trailers, and 22 personnel).

- Always use numerals (not words) to describe time and measurements (3 days, 2 years, 19 miles).

- Capitalize only the first letter of the month when listing dates and use the same date format throughout (1 Apr 10, 31 Dec 10, etc)

- When listing dollar amounts, use either the dollar sign ($) or the word, dollars, not both.

- When listing office designators, use a dash (S-1, G-6, etc)

- Use two spaces following a period when starting a new sentence.

- Use only common Army abbreviations that are understood by everyone. Spell the abbreviation out the first time it is used (if space allows) and, if the abbreviation is used more than once on the same page, list the abbreviation in parenthesis after the first occurrence.

- Capitalize operations and use upper and lower case for exercises (Operation IRAQI FREEDOM, Exercise Anvil Tree)

- Do not list the period of the award or unit in the citation block. This information is already on the form and the space in the citation block is limited.

- Use upper and lower case in the Proposed Citation block and enter at least four lines.

ACHIEVEMENT #1 As a petroleum specialist, SPC Smith performed the duties of HAZCOM. He organized and put into effect a petroleum storage and issue facility, a collection point for hazardous materials. His actions cleared the way for base units to comply with OSHA standards for the first time.
ACHIEVEMENT #2 In addition to his duties as a petroleum specialist for the motor pool, SPC Smith contributed his knowledge of his secondary MOS, vehicle maintenance, to help perform and assist in the completion of many inspections under the motor pool's Quality Assurance program.
ACHIEVEMENT #3 As a Light Wheel Vehicle Mechanic, SPC Smith did an outstanding job of performing and assisting on over 200 vehicle services and repairs. His repairs produced the best sustainment rate in 3 years.
ACHIEVEMENT #4 SPC Smith was runner-up for Soldier of the Quarter and won Soldier of the Month this reporting period. In addition, the promotion board recommended he be promoted to the rank of Sergeant.
PROPOSED CITATION While deployed in support of Operation Iraqi Freedom as a petroleum specialist, SPC Smith immediately saw the need for and established the first hazardous waste collection point bringing order and better working conditions to a chaotic environment. In addition to his regular duties, SPC Smith aided the Vehicle Maintenance shop in the repair and service of over 220 critical vehicles. His valiant efforts produced the lowest vehicle breakdown rate in three years and reflect credit upon himself and the United States Army.

ACHIEVEMENT #1 Despite a lack of supervision or guidance, SPC Smith performed his duties above and beyond expectations. His technical expertise and leadership abilities contributed to the success of the unit's aviation operations tempo during Operation Golden Coyote 2010. His support of this critical endeavor directly enhanced readiness.
ACHIEVEMENT #2 SPC Smith efficiently managed four FARPs daily and cold/hot refuel operations for over 5,500 aircraft during OIF 10 without error or incident. His focused efforts to safely integrate with flightline operations were directly responsible for the air field's impeccable safety record.
ACHIEVEMENT #3 Managed the receipt, storage, transport, and issue of over 1.5 million gallons of JP8 in support of vital combat aviation operations during OIF 10 within allowable gain/loss limits. In addition, he assisted in the training of the squad to ensure all Soldiers were proficient in all POL operations.
ACHIEVEMENT #4 Demonstrated initiative by volunteering for and adapting to frequent changes while preparing for the M2 and M249 range. While at the range, his sense of fairness, good judgment, and communication skills effectively helped peers maintain qualification and ensured range safety.
PROPOSED CITATION For meritorious achievement while assigned as POL Specialist during the Global War on Terror in support of Operation Iraqi Freedom. Specialist Smith's support and professionalism during refueling operations were vital to the success of the mission. His communication skills, leadership, and ability to perform made him an invaluable team member. His superior performance is in keeping with the finest traditions of military service and reflects great credit upon himself, this command, and the United States Army.

ACHIEVEMENT #1 Selected from among peers to serve as First Cook during the Connelly large dining facility competition, he devoted long hours over five days preparing and performing for inspectors. His efforts garnered recognition for best lighting and sanitation seen to date.
ACHIEVEMENT #2 Before deployment to FOB Echo, SPC Smith used initiative to stage and inventory all convoy vehicles. Working as a Food Service Specialist, he did an outstanding job of arranging and assisting in preparation of meals for over 250 Solders twice a day during the entire deployment. Despite being under strength, the Food service section met all meal requirements.
ACHIEVEMENT #3 Helped organize unscheduled food service for temporary forces; he displayed efficiency, skill, and leadership while mentoring the lower enlisted in practical organization of expedient field kitchen service. His attention to detail resulted in a safe worksite and his culinary skills also helped to maintain and reinforce the morale and readiness of the deployed force.
ACHIEVEMENT #4 SPC Smith, responsible for feeding over 250 519th MP Battalion Soldiers in a field environment, maintained numerous outside lines and was integral to the orderly and efficient delivery of over 2,000 meals. He displayed a high degree of professionalism, technical expertise, and dedication to duty. Soldier also demonstrated a tireless commitment to excellence and consistently achieved high standards.
PROPOSED CITATION For meritorious service while assigned as Food Service Specialist in support of Operation IRAQI FREEDOM. During this period, through foresight, planning, and determination, he accomplished all assigned tasks quickly and effectively. SPC Smith's relentless drive, initiative, and perseverance earned wide recognition and inspired his peers and subordinates to strive for excellence. Working long, arduous hours, he has contributed greatly to the success of numerous operations. His commendable performance is in keeping with the finest traditions of military service and reflect credit upon himself, his unit, and the United States Army.

Citation Example

SPECIALIST JOHN SMITH

311th Base Support Battalion

For outstanding achievement as a Petroleum Specialist, 311th Base Support Battalion, while deployed in support of Operation Iraqi Freedom. On arrival, SPC Smith immediately recognized the need for and established the first hazardous waste collection point in Ahn Bar Province bringing order to a chaotic environment. His actions streamlined operations and brought the battalion into OSHA compliance for the first time. In addition, Specialist Smith aided the Vehicle Maintenance shop in the repair of over 220 vehicles. His valiant efforts produced the lowest vehicle breakdown rate in three years and bring great credit upon himself, the 311th BSB, and the United States Army.

PERIOD: 25 MAR 2007 TO 24 APR 2008

Note that certificate citations for the Army Achievement Medal are limited to six lines. (Each line in this book is roughly equal to half of one line on the certificate.)

The citation for the AAM is typed directly into the DA Form 638. Later, the Commander's staff will transfer the text to DA Form 4980–18 Army Achievement Medal Certificate.

Army policy does not restrict the use of abbreviations and acronyms in award citations. However, due to the inherent historical value of the award certificate and the acts or service it represents, it is imperative that it be prepared with care so that its appearance is professional and dignified. It is also recommended that only the most commonly known abbreviations and acronyms be used in the citation.

The abbreviation/acronym should be spelled out the first time it's used and followed by the abbreviation/acronym in parenthesis. If the abbreviation or acronym is used only once, after spelling it out initially, there is no need to list the abbreviation afterwards.

Certificates should include a brief descriptive narrative but should not be so brief as to distract from its meaning and should be prepared on a letter quality printer or equivalent.

AAM Citation Examples

Citation to accompany the award of the Army Achievement Medal

For superior and unflagging support to the 449th Inland Cargo Transfer Company. Your ability to adapt quickly to an evolving, ever-changing environment under austere conditions whenever it was needed is commendable. The long hours and dedication you provided were instrumental to the success of the exercise. Your professionalism brings great credit upon you, the 449th Inland Cargo Transfer Company, and the United States Army.

For exceptionally outstanding achievement in having attained a perfect score of 100 percent on the skill qualification test. Staff Sergeant Smith's outstanding performance significantly contributes to combat readiness and reflects great credit upon himself and the United States Army.

For outstanding achievement as a tank turret mechanic during the Battalion's Level I tank gunnery. Your exemplary dedication to duty and technical expertise contributed significantly to D Company's maintenance success. This outstanding performance reflects great credit upon you, the Devil Dogs, and the United States Army.

For outstanding achievement as Orderly Room NCO, 411th BSB, while deployed in support of Operation Iraqi Freedom. SGT Smith tracked and processed over 150 unscheduled leaves and passes while maintaining a 95% manning rate. Under shifting command and conditions, she organized and prepared the unit for redeployment and reintegration into central region upon completion of their 15 month deployment with zero loss of accountability. The accomplishments of SGT Smith bring great credit upon herself, the 411th BSB, and the United States Army.

For exceptionally meritorious service while serving as the Battalion S-4 Officer, Headquarters 69th Ordnance Battalion during the period of 5 March 2002 to 20 June 2004. His outstanding initiative, leadership, and logistics abilities produced greatly improved supply, maintenance, and financial programs and led to a twenty percent increase in equipment serviceability rates for the Battalion. His skillful administration of supply and logistics matters resulted in the Battalion's successful completion of its Army Training and Evaluation Programs and two major field exercises. Captain Smith's outstanding achievements and devotion to duty reflect favorably upon himself, the 69th Ordnance Battalion, and the 1st Armored Division.

For meritorious service while assigned as assistant gunner and gunner from 15 January 2003 to 15 August 2004 in the Bravo Company 60mm mortar section. Private Smith displayed fortitude, dedication, and skill during the Multi-national Force rotation, the Battalion MORTEP and mortar live fire exercise, and the Brigade Pre-Ranger Course. Private Smith's performance reflects great credit upon himself, 2d Battalion, 3d Infantry, and the United States Army.

For exceptionally meritorious service as a crewchief during the period 5 April 2004 through 25 May 2004. Throughout this period Private First Class Smith demonstrated superior occupational skills and technical knowledge within the Kiowa maintenance field. Additionally, Private First Class Smith's motivation inspired his peers and contributed significantly towards a 100% aircraft operational readiness rate. Private First Class Smith has distinguished himself as a competent Soldier whose achievements reflect credit upon himself and this unit.

For exceptional knowledge and professionalism which resulted in your selection as Fort Stewart's Noncommissioned Officer of the Second Quarter, fiscal year 2009. Your outstanding leadership qualities and attitude in the accomplishment of assigned duties reflect great credit upon you and the United States Army.

For exceptionally meritorious service as a Unit Readiness Noncommissioned Officer deployed to the Gulf of Mexico in response to an emergency environmental crisis. His devotion to duty, loyalty, and exemplary teamwork led to the successful sustainment of recovery operations in support of Operation Deepwater Horizon. His dedication and performance reflects great credit upon himself, the 1165th Military Police Company, and the United States Army.

For exemplary performance during the Battalion Field Training Exercise 7-11 April 2008. His motivation, initiative, dedication, and technical knowledge were key elements in the Battalion's success. His performance brings great credit upon himself, his unit, the 101st Aviation Regiment , and the United States Army.

The Army Commendation Medal

The documents listed below are all you need for submitting an Army Commendation Medal package.

Ref AR600-8-22, Military Awards

The ARCOM is awarded to any member of the Armed Forces of the United States who distinguishes himself or herself by heroism, meritorious achievement or meritorious service.

Awards of the ARCOM may be made for acts of valor performed under circumstances described above which are of lesser degree than required for award of the Bronze Star Medal. These acts may involve aerial flight. The ARCOM may be awarded for acts of noncombatant-related heroism which does not meet the requirements for an award of the Soldier's Medal.

The Army Commendation Medal may be awarded with the bronze V device for heroic acts or valorous deeds which are not of the level to warrant award of the Distinguished Flying Cross or the Bronze Star Medal with "V" device.

Ref AR600-8-22 Para 6-5: "the "V" device was also authorized for wear on the Air Medal and Army Commendation Medal for heroic acts or valorous deeds not warranting awards of the Distinguished Flying Cross or the Bronze Star Medal with "V" device."

How to Complete the DA Form 638

The requirements for submitting someone for a medal, whether it's a Commendation Medal or a Bronze Star, are largely the same but there are some differences. They all require the filling out of the DA Form 638 and for some medals, like the Achievement Medal and the Commendation Medal, that's all that's required. But for the heavyweights, like the Commendation Medal with V Device, Bronze Star, etc, more support is required. To avoid confusion, these instructions will address only the Army Commendation Medal.

Block 1. Fill in the office information of the next office above the recommender in the Chain of Command. This is the office with approval authority.

Block 2. Enter the recommender's office information.

Blocks 3-7. Self Explanatory

Block 8. Fill in the individual's previous awards. The Army Service Ribbon (ASR), Korean Defense Service Medal (KDSM), Kuwait Liberation Medal (KULIBM), and Southwest Asia Service Medal (SWASM) are service medals and should not be listed.

Block 9. Enter the Service and Component of the person being recommended. Use the following:

Services	Component
USA - Army	Act - Active Duty
USMC - Marine Corps	Res - Reserve Forces
USN - Navy	NG - National Guard
USAF - Air Force	

Block 10. Enter the award being recommended to include number of award/oak leaf cluster

Block 11-19. Self Explanatory

Block 20. For the ARCOM, using the space provided in the DA Form 638, fill in the Soldier's achievements or meritorious service using bullet format.

Block 21. Enter the ARCOM citation.

Block 22. Staff Section Admin Clerk should sign and date verifying individual is eligible for the recommended award.

Block 23-25. Fill in intermediate commanders as appropriate.

Block 26.

a. ORDERS ISSUING AUTHORITY

b. CDR, MNC-I APO AE 09999

e. JOHN Q. PUBLIC

f. COL
g. COMMANDING

Block 27.

a. HQ, MNC-I APO AE 09999

Block 28.

a. JOHN SMITH
b. MSG
c. Chief, CJ1 Personnel Actions

Block 29-30. Leave blank

Block 31. Distribution

1-SOLDIER

1-UNIT

1-FILE

1-OMPF

Award Bullet Examples

According to AR 600-8-22, Military Awards, narrative description of meritorious service or achievement for awards of the Army Commendation Medal will be limited to the space allowed on the DA Form 638. This means that the only justification or support required for award of the medal is what can be typed or handwritten in the Achievement blocks on the DA Form 638; no separate attachment is required. The DA Form 638 contains four separate blocks for listing individual accomplishments, each block being limited to four lines. Use bullet format when describing accomplishments in these blocks.

See the guidance listed in the Army Achievement Medal section for general administrative requirements.

ACHIEVEMENT #1 SFC Smith served as Convoy Commander, conducting over 80 Combat Logistic Patrols and driving over 5,000 miles accident free. His expertise and willingness to execute combat logistic patrols throughout Northern Iraq along MSRs and ASRs contributed to the team's overall success, and ensured all supplies, equipment, and personnel returned from every mission.
ACHIEVEMENT #2 SFC Smith was directly responsible for the Iraqis' sustainment and initial fielding of over $3 million of equipment. Through his dedication and persistence he guaranteed the team's overall success as a Border Transition Team at one of Iraq's most important Ports of Entry. His leadership and expertise improved the logistics capabilities of senior Iraqi Commanders.
ACHIEVEMENT #3 SFC Smith served as Logistics NCO for Port of Entry 227. He assumed responsibility for the team's Property Book containing over $3 million worth of equipment. He supervised five NCOs and focused special emphasis on accountability and maintenance of team equipment. Close interaction with team members ensured team equipment was continually at 100% readiness.
ACHIEVEMENT #4 He mentored other NCOs, trained Gun Truck Commanders, ensured all team members were cross-trained and capable of all tasks within their crew vehicle. His dedication to mission safety and his soldiers' safety earned an unwavering trust and loyalty from his subordinates and other Non Commissioned Officers.
PROPOSED CITATION For exceptionally meritorious service as Detachment Logistics NCO and Convoy Commander for POETT 227 from 22 January 2007 to 30 December 2007. SFC Smith's actions were directly responsible for the sustainment of his unit and Iraqi support. His continuous determination toward self-sufficiency ensured not only mission-readiness but the survival of his unit and his Soldiers. SFC Smith's actions bring great credit upon himself, the 214th TSG, and the United States Army

ACHIEVEMENT #1 Served as Operations NCO for the Readiness Group's Mobilization and Demobilization Assistance Teams at Ft Rucker. While in this position, SFC Smith was responsible for the training and subsequent mobilization and demobilization of 24 Reserve Component units supporting over 3,000 Soldiers.
ACHIEVEMENT #2 As an action officer for the Readiness Group Commander responsible for identifying and documenting problems associated with mobilization in support of Desert Shield and Desert Storm, SFC Smith wrote several influential After Action Reports that addressed and resolved many major issues.
ACHIEVEMENT #3 Assigned as NCOIC of Ordnance Branch Mobilization Assistance Team, SFC Smith contributed to the immediate readiness of 24 maintenance and ammunition logistics units across the Southeastern district. In addition, his assistance of the 411th Ordnance Group and subordinate units in preparing for a demanding Operational Readiness Evaluation schedule was a major factor in their success.
ACHIEVEMENT #4 SFC Smith improved the mission capability of the Ordnance Team by increasing the number of qualified NCOs and Soldiers capable of assisting assigned units by increasing individual training and developing in-house training programs that addressed mobilization, OREs, and other topics specific to regional support.
PROPOSED CITATION For outstanding meritorious service as NCOIC, ordnance branch mobilization assistance team, Readiness Group Redstone. Sergeant First Class Smith's expertise as an experienced logistician and his commitment to the total Army ensured the immediate readiness of reserve component maintenance and ammunition support units throughout the Southeast. His service reflects great credit upon himself, Readiness Group Redstone, and the United States Army.

ACHIEVEMENT #1 As Platoon Sergeant, suggested and implemented changes to the SECFOR SOP and enforced strict adherence which led to the safe completion of more than 20,000 vehicle and 50,000 personnel searches while continuing to work diligently to improve base security.
ACHIEVEMENT #2 Chosen to serve as Acting First Sergeant during his absence; ensured compliance with Army regulations and SOP, maintained Soldier discipline and morale, and held unit and Soldier performance to the highest standard. He continued to complete his daily duties as Platoon Sergeant while serving as Acting First Sergeant.
ACHIEVEMENT #3 Met and exceeded his responsibilities as Platoon Sergeant by, in addition to his daily taskings, assuming the roles of BDOC NCOIC and BDOC Liaison between sister services and Kuwaiti military personnel. Assisted UMO with packing and documenting movement to Kuwait.
ACHIEVEMENT #4 A dedicated instructor, he oversaw battalion MOB training requirements culminating in 100% trained status; developed PMCS for equipment and instructed soldiers on maintenance and troubleshooting of communications equipment; successfully completed three theatre retrograde missions as the daytime Security Force Platoon Leader.
PROPOSED CITATION For meritorious service as Platoon Sergeant, 2nd Bn, 214th FA. Staff Sergeant Smith's expertise as an experienced leader and his commitment to the Army ensured the mission readiness of the 214th Field Artillery. His service reflects great credit on himself, the 2nd Battalion, 214th Field Artillery, and the United States Army.

Citation Example

STAFF SERGEANT SMITH

JOINT TASK FORCE

For exceptionally meritorious service while assigned as crew chief in support of military operations against terrorist aggression in the republic of Afghanistan. During this period, he astutely surmounted extremely adverse conditions to consistently obtain superior results. Through diligence and determination, he accomplished every task quickly and efficiently. His unrelenting loyalty, initiative, and perseverance brought him wide acclaim and inspired his peers and subordinates to strive for maximum achievement. Selflessly working long and arduous hours, he has contributed greatly to the success of the multinational effort. His commendable performance is in keeping with the finest traditions of military service and reflects credit upon himself, his unit, and the United States Army.

PERIOD: 25 MAR 2007 TO 24 APR 2008

Note that certificate citations for the Meritorious Service Medal, Army Commendation Medal and Army Achievement Medal are limited to six lines.

The citation for the ARCOM is typed directly into the DA Form 638. Later, the Commander's staff will transfer the text to DA Form 4980–14 Army Commendation Medal Certificate.

Army policy does not restrict the use of abbreviations and acronyms in award citations. However, due to the inherent historical value of the award certificate and the acts or service it represents, it is imperative that it be prepared with care so that its appearance is professional and dignified. It is also recommended that only the most commonly known abbreviations and acronyms be used in the citation. The abbreviation/acronym should be spelled out the first time and followed by the abbreviation/acronym in parenthesis. Certificates should include a brief descriptive narrative and should not be so brief as to distract from its meaning, and should be prepared on a letter quality printer or equivalent.

ARCOM Citation Examples

Citation to accompany the award of the Army Commendation Medal

For superior and unflagging service to the 363rd Quarter Master Battalion. Sergeant Smith's dedication and commitment to success make him an outstanding leader. SGT Smith, through his actions, has gained the respect of Soldiers and leaders at all levels. His determination toward self-development and the improvement of the organization set the example for all enlisted Soldiers and non-commissioned and commissioned officers. SGT Smith's actions bring great credit upon himself, the 363rd QM BN, the US Army Reserve, and the United States Army.

For vital support of the USADENTAC fiscal year 2009 close out. As the Supply NCOIC for Dental Clinic #1, you provided critical technical support to the organization by timely management of expenditures in excess of $800,000. Your contributions serve as a sterling example of the effective and judicious use of organizational funds and resulted in continuous pro-active solutions ensuring the availability of non-expendable, durable and expendable supplies and equipment. Your actions produced a zero balance of all funds prior to Army mandated fiscal year closeout and ensured the continued success of the mission of the USADENTAC. Your actions as Supply NCOIC, Dental Clinic #1, bring great credit upon yourself, the U.S. Army Materiel Command, and the United States Army.

For exceptionally meritorious service while assigned as a Counter Rocket Artillery Mortar Sense and Warn Team Leader from 10 August 2007 through 2 Jan 2008. As a member of the Multinational Division Center South Sense and Warn section at Camp Bravo, Ad Diwaniyah, Iraq, Sergeant Smith played a vital role in the success of the mission. When an IDF attack disabled the main generators powering the Tactical Operations Center and supporting radar system, SGT Smith took immediate action. With no radar coverage and still under Red conditions, SGT Smith moved to the Special Forces compound and completely assembled and activated their Counter Mortar Radar. This provided Camp Bravo with temporary radar coverage for 12 hours until the main generators were repaired. SGT Smith's dedication and devotion to duty is in keeping with the finest traditions of the Army and reflects great credit upon himself, the Strike First Battalion, and the United States Army.

For exceptionally meritorious service in support of military operations against terrorist aggression in the Republic of Afghanistan. During this period, despite adverse conditions and a lack of support he worked diligently to prepare for and accomplish all assigned missions. Through careful analysis and route planning, every mission, whether mounted or dismounted, was achieved on time and with unmatched results. His fierce determination to overcome all obstacles to mission success inspired his team and impressed his superiors. Selflessly assuming responsibility for both his team's and higher headquarters' tasking, he has contributed greatly to the success of the multinational effort. His commendable performance is in keeping with the finest traditions of the military service and reflects credit upon himself, his unit, and the United States Army.

For meritorious service as Support Operations Sergeant for the 3d Corps Support Command (COSCOM), V Corps, Germany. As Support Operations Sergeant, he deployed in support of both OPERATIONS IRAQI and ENDURING FREEDOM. Displaying great courage, he personally led reconnaissance teams on several missions into enemy territory by ground and air to locate and identify high-value, non-mission capable equipment requiring retrograding. In addition, his leadership and expertise was key to the relocation of V Corps integrated headquarters over 1,000 kilometers with no loss of communication. Furthermore, he spearheaded the analysis of damage to several of the attack helicopter regiment's aircraft after a major enemy attack, coordinated the delivery of critical repair parts and arranged the required depot maintenance which led to 100% mission restoral in less than ten days. The distinctive accomplishments of Master Sergeant Smith reflect credit upon himself, V Corps, and the United States Army.

For meritorious achievement as Team Leader, Charlie Company, 2-275th Infantry, Sergeant Smith displayed leadership and competence by taking the initiative to research and implement a program to outfit the company's vehicles with long range antennae. The antennae were vital to improving communication between vehicles on combat logistic patrols across dangerous and unsecured terrain. With the regulation antennae, communications between vehicles, across distances as short as three miles, was intermittent. SGT Smith spent more than 100 hours testing and configuring antennae until a practical solution was found. The long range antennae improved Charlie company logistic patrols communications and improved personnel safety and mission accomplishment. SGT Smith's performance brings great credit upon himself, his unit, and the United States Army.

For meritorious service as Information Systems Analyst, 25th Infantry Division, U.S. Army Garrison, Hawaii, from 11 December 2003 to 30 April 2006. During this period, Sergeant Smith repaired more than 200 small computers base-wide and saved the government over 100,000 dollars in repair costs. He excelled at customer education and provided 12 software classes to joint service members saving the government an estimated 55,000 dollars in tuition costs. Sergeant Smith's assistance to an Air Force Engineering and Installation team during the cutover of the communications center's switching system, which routed critical command and control message traffic, ensured a successful conversion with zero downtime. In addition, his efforts in tracking and removing several computer viruses isolated the loss of data and saved the entire installation from a catastrophic communications outage. Sergeant Smith's performance brings great credit upon himself, the 25th Infantry Division, and the United States Army.

For exceptionally meritorious service as a Communication Electronics Staff Officer and Headquarters Company Commander, 214th Engineer Combat Battalion (Heavy) from 11 November 2006 to 14 May 2008. Captain Smith's astute guidance resulted in excellent communications support to his battalion during an ARTEP, CPX, and an eleven month construction project. His outstanding management skills ensured continued mission accomplishment of this diverse company and its consolidated dining facility. His ability to balance his responsibilities as Commander, CESO, and Dining Facility Supervisor resulted in maximum readiness for the unit. Captain Smith's performance of duty brings distinct credit upon himself, the 22nd Engineer Brigade, and the United States Army.

Generic Award Bullets

Sometimes it's hard to come up with a bullet for that fourth block on the DA Form 638. Below is a short collection of bullet comments that are common to most MOS and duty positions. Hopefully one or more of these will remind you of one of your accomplishments that you had previously overlooked.

On short notice, reacted and put together an Honor Guard detail for the funeral of a retired member.

Created a successful APFT program; ensured 100% pass rate for all soldiers taking PT test during Annual Training.

SPC Smith planned and executed three Warrior Training Tasks (WTT) with a 100% pass rate.

Soldier is proactive in performing duties prior to becoming a directive.

This Soldier's professional guidance and leadership was the ideal example of a Soldier and a leader to all of First Squad during the CAPEX.

Demonstrated exemplary leadership and competency while activated for annual training.

Identified specific warrior task training and leadership development skills essential for unit competency and exhibited exceptional proficiency in delivering them.

Showed superior leadership by training and mentoring soldiers during Warrior Task Training and continuously offered his experience and various skills to those in need.

Actions significantly enhanced the combat readiness and support of deployed Soldiers and Soldier systems supporting operations in Iraq and Afghanistan.

Volunteered in the 2008 Para-Olympic law enforcement run from Atlanta to Alexandria covering over 25 miles.

Performed exceptionally and far beyond his skill level and endured long hours of work dedicated to accomplishing the unit's mission during annual training 2010.

Spent 10 hours mentoring elementary school students; imparted importance of academics and right decisions.

Put together a hands-on training module which contributed to the overall success and completion of DAGR training.

Trained squad during the Combatives Class in preparation for the Best Warrior Competition 2010.

Assisted local community in crisis and demonstrated what the National Guard does as Citizen Soldiers.

Dedication and commitment have proven him to be a model Soldier that sets the standard and is a fine example of what a lower enlisted Soldier should be.

Outstanding performance and dedication to duty were a major factor in the success of the Welcome Home Warrior ceremony and Change of Command Ceremony.

Set the example for peers to emulate by meticulously maintaining assigned vehicles to 10/20 standards and ensuring mission readiness; commitment to mission accomplishment contributed to the successful execution of Brigade's mission.

In addition to his regular duties, SPC Smith has also proven to be a excellent source of information for his fellow enlisted Soldiers ensuring that they have the right information, follow the right procedures, and are properly prepared.

As acting platoon sergeant, SGT Smith distinguished himself by serving two levels higher than his rank; his leadership and technical and tactical proficiency ensured the successful training of 15 Soldiers in 10 Army Warrior Tasks.

Was responsible for maintaining 100% accountability of all assigned equipment, worth in excess of 1.5 million dollars; careful attention to detail proved to be a vital tool in making sure the Task Force exceeded its assigned mission.

Mentored and trained others; preparing detailed orientation classes; demonstrated outstanding leadership skills.

As a Rear Detachment NCOIC, performed his duties with distinction; his professionalism and devotion to duty played a key role in the success of the Rear Detachment.

Volunteered numerous hours with the MWR facilities to build Army relations with the civilian population.

Superior performer and superb manager identifying and fixing problems with mission preparation that resulted in cutting our mission prep time by 25%.

Volunteered within both the community and the Wisconsin Army National Guard; did an outstanding job of representing not only 2nd Bn/214th FA but all Soldiers.

Went above and beyond his duty by performing QRF operations; with little time to prepare, executed the mission with precision and the highest level of motivation; all standards of the mission were met or exceeded.

SFC Smith worked as a Range Safety and as the primary Tower Safety for countless small arms ranges, supervising more than 1000 Soldiers with no safety incidents.

Directed unit and active duty personnel as team leader during wartime deployment greatly improving contingency knowledge; surpassing all expectations, SSG Smith's hands-on leadership was the catalyst for the entire effort.

SPC Smith researched and delivered Land Navigation instruction at an understandable level and created a comfortable and effective learning environment.

Although not a supply sergeant, SSG Smith helped supply the 123rd Rear Detachment with the supplies needed for new soldiers and to conduct daily operations.

Demonstrated outstanding performance, professional competence, and selfless devotion to duty and enhanced operational support and ensured mission accomplishment while enabling the Soldiers of 2nd SFG to deploy around the world.

SPC Smith became a subject matter expert in all technical and tactical matters related to not only his duty position, but of those above and below him.

His constant commitment to improving his personnel resulted in ten Soldiers advancing at least one pay grade

Having great knowledge of Land Navigation, he was chosen from among his peers to be a guide and help Soldiers navigate when lost; was also selected to provide LMTV support for the Battalion Warrior Forge exercise.

With no formal training, became 3d Platoon's subject matter expert and authority on three new communications systems; he worked tirelessly to become proficient on the new systems and get them working and was directly responsible for successful communications throughout the exercise.

During field training exercises, MSG Smith stood with or above his peers and provided direct training and mentoring to Soldiers and other NCOs that resulted in not only their success, but the overall success of the unit's mission.

Performed duties as Platoon Sergeant while deployed in Iraq; assisted, advised, and maintained accountability in the management of many major projects; maintained a high level of military leadership as well as technical expertise that ensured the success of the unit's overall mission.

Maintained a high level of safety on all platoon missions; despite a demanding schedule and limited support, all were completed without unnecessary injuries or fatalities.

Was responsible for the relocation, inventory, and transport of unit property during the relocation process; her attention to detail helped achieve 100% accountability of all property.

SSG Smith resourced, coordinated, and trained and certified 12 Soldiers in Ramadi on the Iraq theater BIP course; improved Soldier qualification and readiness.

SPC Smith was selected above 13 of her peers to perform duties as a Battalion mail room clerk; while performing duties outside of her primary MOS, maintained 100% accountability of mail for 550 Soldiers in the Bn.

SSG Smith's actions and example were directly responsible for the success of his team during annual training; his continuous dedication and determination ensured mission readiness and enhanced operational support.

SSG Smith conducted two NBC chambers and a CIP for 2 Companies that resulted in the Battalion being in 100% compliance with FORSCOM annual training requirements and ready for upcoming deployment.

Performed every mission and every task outside his area of expertise with enthusiasm and a positive attitude and an unmatched skill set; SPC Smith continually volunteered for missions during and after his required work time.

SFC Smith stepped up and assumed the role and responsibility for duties above his pay grade; SFC Smith identified deficiencies in the company's counseling of Soldiers and developed a tracker to identify and bring the company up to date with all required counseling.

Responsible for the accountability and maintenance of equipment valued in excess of one million dollars throughout his tenure as Platoon Sergeant; he ensured the platoon's equipment was properly inventoried, accounted for, and packed in preparation for numerous training events and deployments in support of Operation Iraqi Freedom.

SFC Smith demonstrated exceptional performance as a Brigade and Group level Operations Sergeant; he expertly supported numerous missions as the S3/Operations

Sergeant for deploying units while participating in numerous CPX, MRX, and BCST training events.

While participating in Combat Logistic Patrols, SGT Smith performed above and beyond his normal duties; he learned how to operate and troubleshoot the AN/PRC-145 (MBITR) radio and use the Simple Key Loader (SKL); ensured all convoy tractor/trailers had communications.

SGT Smith demonstrated responsibility and initiative while assigned as duty driver during the Leadership Reaction Course, delivering a professional and efficient performance under rapidly shifting circumstances.

Played a key role in the success of the platoon's mission; SPC Smith demonstrated exceptional resourcefulness and dedication to duty. His hard work, positive attitude, and willingness to accept additional responsibilities were vital to standing up Bravo Company.

SGT Smith demonstrated exceptional resourcefulness and dedication to duty; SGT Smith's tact, hard work, positive attitude toward his job and willingness to accept additional responsibilities were particularly noteworthy.

SGT Smith went above and beyond the call of duty, using his personal time to help his fellow Soldiers; helped two Soldiers pass their APFT, exceeding the Army standard by over forty points.

As a member of the Camp Arifjan's Quick Reaction Force, SGT Smith conducted over 50 force protection patrols which ensured the safety and security of Camp Arifjan personnel and its mission.

Generic Citations

The best citations describe exactly what a Soldier accomplished but sometimes, when that information is not available, we have to resort to general descriptions of the individual's notable service. The citations below are meant to help on those occasions.

For exceptionally meritorious service as Chemical, Biological, Radiological, Nuclear Non-Commissioned Officer, 519th Military Police Battalion from 1 January 2008 to 31 December 2009. Throughout his 22 years of service, Sergeant First Class Smith has distinguished himself by exceptional duty performance in positions of importance and responsibility. During his career, Sergeant Smith exhibited extraordinary leadership, technical, and training skills which consistently enhanced the combat readiness of numerous Army units. His career has been marked by true professionalism and dedication and reflects great credit upon himself, the 519th Military Police Battalion, and the United States Army.

For meritorious service as Aviation Life Support Equipment NCO, 214th Aviation Training Assistance Team, while deployed to Kuwait in support of Operation Enduring Freedom. Sergeant Smith's dedication and outstanding performance were significant and directly responsible for the operational success of the mission. His professionalism and unwavering commitment to duty were an example to his peers and provided inspiration under the most austere of conditions. The distinctive accomplishments of Sergeant Smith reflect credit upon himself and the United States Army.

For meritorious service as NCOIC, Flight Operations, while assigned to Joint Sustainment Command, Afghanistan from 3 January 2009 to 29 Dec 2009. Sergeant Smith's dedication and commitment to his troops and the success of the operation make him an outstanding leader. Sergeant Smith, through his actions, has gained the respect of Soldiers and Non-Commissioned Officers at all levels. His determination toward self-development and the improvement of the organization set the example for all enlisted members and Non-Commissioned Officers. The distinctive accomplishments of Sergeant Smith reflect credit upon himself and the United States Army.

For meritorious service while assigned as a Security Force Member and Vehicle Commander in support of military operations against terrorist aggression in the Republic of Afghanistan. During this period, Sergeant First Class Smith surmounted extremely adverse conditions to consistently obtain superior results. Through diligence and determination, and despite a lack of personnel and equipment, he accomplished all assigned tasks quickly and efficiently. His unrelenting loyalty, initiative, and perseverance brought him wide recognition and inspired his peers and subordinates to strive for maximum achievement. Selflessly working long hours, he has contributed greatly to the success of the multinational effort. The distinctive accomplishments of Sergeant Smith are in keeping with the finest traditions of military service and reflect great credit upon himself and the United States Army.

For meritorious service while assigned to the 358th Civil Affairs Brigade, Riverside, California, from 4 January 2008 to 21 March 2010. During this period, Staff Sergeant Smith consistently displayed exemplary professionalism and initiative in obtaining outstanding results. His rapid assessment and solution to numerous problems greatly enhanced the Brigade's capability and effectiveness, at home station and while deployed. Despite significant and continuing changes to the unit's organizational structure and severe time-constraints, he consistently performed his duties in a resolute and efficient manner. His loyalty, diligence, and devotion to duty contributed significantly to the successful accomplishment of the Army mission during this rotation of Operation Iraqi Freedom and were in keeping with the highest traditions of military service. The distinctive accomplishments of Staff Sergeant Smith reflect credit upon himself and the United States Army.

For exceptionally meritorious service as Operations Advisor, Soldier Readiness Processing Center, Republic of Afghanistan. Sergeant Smith made a tremendous impact on the proficiency and increased state of readiness of troops entering the theater. Sergeant Smith's organizational abilities dramatically enhanced the planning, coordination, and execution of the multi-national force deployment during a very operationally demanding period. Sergeant Smith was instrumental in the development of a cohesive staff capable of rapid and effective military decision-making. His organization and leadership was one of the most significant contributing factors to the success of Task Force Anvil Tree resulting in over 250 Soldiers being trained and in-processed in less than a week. The distinctive accomplishments of Sergeant Smith reflect great credit upon himself and the United States Army.

For meritorious service as NCOIC, 143rd Expeditionary Sustainment Command, Joint Sustainment Command-Afghanistan. He consistently manifested exemplary professionalism and initiative in supporting over five thousand deployed Soldiers. His rapid assessment and innovative solutions to numerous logistical problems greatly enhanced the allied effectiveness against a determined and aggressive enemy. Despite many adversities and under the harshest of conditions, he consistently performed his duties in a resolute and efficient manner. The distinctive accomplishments of Staff Sergeant Smith reflect great credit upon himself and the United States Army.

For Meritorious Service as crewmember, E Company, 12th Engineering Battalion from 16 September 2009 to 9 July 2010. During his deployment to Senegal, Sergeant Smith demonstrated outstanding qualities of initiative and motivation. His experience and proficiency in day to day operations was unsurpassed. His vigilance and knowledge were key to the Company's successful participation in numerous exercises. Sergeant Smith's expertise was repeatedly demonstrated by the exceptional condition and operational readiness of his equipment and in the continuous advancement of the mission. Sergeant Smith's performance reflects great credit upon himself, the 12th Engineering Battalion, and the United States Army.

For exceptionally meritorious service while serving as a Fire Direction Center Computer during Operation Iraqi Freedom. Specialist Doe's outstanding dedication to duty during combat operations contributed to the overwhelming success of the command's critical mission in support of the dedicated actions of the multi-national forces in Iraq. His actions are in keeping with the finest traditions of military service and reflect great credit upon himself, the 4th Brigade Combat Team, 1st Armored Division and the United States Army.

For meritorious achievement as acting Human Resource Sergeant. Your voluntary assumption of duties and selfless dedication to a vastly improved deployed Brigade Headquarters posture in only six short months are a great credit to you and the United States Army Reserve.

For exceptionally meritorious service during the period 10 April 2002 to 25 June 2005 while serving as the Operations Sergeant, 107th Engineer Battalion. A gifted staff NCO, he skillfully applied doctrine and theory to real world problems, keeping abreast of all actions affecting the resources and readiness of the 107th Engineer Battalion and providing support to the multinational force. An innovative and concerned Soldier, he focused his efforts on training junior members and on improving efficiency in the Battalion Tactical Operations Center. He successfully transitioned control of the forward province from the United States to civilian control, aggressively pursued accountability and vigorous Preventive Maintenance of tactical and leased commercial equipment. Master Sergeant Smith's exemplary performance reflects distinct credit upon himself, the 107th Engineer Battalion, and the United States Army.

Memorandum of Commendation

In addition to the Certificate of Achievement, acts of notable service that do not meet standards required for formal decorations may be recognized with a Memorandum of Commendation/ Appreciation. These should be typed on letterhead. A Memorandum of Commendation/Appreciation is appropriate when an individual demonstrated a highly satisfactory performance.

EXAMPLES

1. I wish to take this opportunity to extend my sincere appreciation for your participation in the static display for the German and Allied Soldiers during the US-led NATO Exercise, Combined Endeavor 2005.

2. The military bearing, responsiveness, and expertise you displayed as a member of a Bradley squad is indicative of a professional attitude, teamwork, and a "can do" attitude. Your outstanding performance reflected great pride on yourself and the 3d Battalion, 51st Air Defense Artillery.

3. General Gunther Teckhaus, Commander of the German 16th Panzer Brigade, stated that, of all the activities that he and his staff attended, the most impressive was that presented by the 3rd Battalion, 51st Air Defense Artillery.

4. Thank you for a professional job well done.

5. A copy of this letter will be placed in your MPRJ.

Signature Block

SUBJECT: Memorandum of Commendation

1. I commend you for achieving the coveted award of Noncommissioned Officer of the Quarter, 2d Quarter, 2009. The Outstanding Noncommissioned Officer of the Quarter Program is conducted at Fort Bliss to promote esprit de corps and to reward enlisted personnel who have exceeded the standards of conduct, military bearing, and other soldierly qualities normally expected of members of the United States Army.

2. To be selected as Noncommissioned Officer of the Quarter is an event in your Army career which you may look upon with pride. Your soldierly appearance, poise, exemplary conduct, mental alertness, and extensive knowledge demonstrated during your appearance before the selection board were judged, by a panel of distinguished military NCOs, to be superior and an example to your peers.

3. I commend you for your efforts. Keep up the fine work.

Signature Block

SUBJECT: Letter of Commendation

1. I would like to take this opportunity to commend your brigade for their recent role in the emplacement of a critical Meybey mobile bridge on the Euphrates River near Camp Ramadi that significantly improved transportation.

2. The mission of hauling bridge components to the bridge site was accomplished in the usual competent manner that is typical of missions undertaken by the 1st Brigade Combat team. I was especially pleased to learn of the part your men played in the actual assembly of the bridge despite unexpected flooding and other obstacles.

3. During initial stages of erection it was difficult for the responsible unit to assemble many men or enough pontoon boats at the erection site due to the condition of the river. Your action in organizing your drivers and support personnel into crews to assist in the bridge assembly was in the finest engineer tradition of cooperation to accomplish an urgent mission. In fact, the esprit and drive of your team enabled them to out-produce other units in similar, competitive tasks.

4. Please convey my admiration, praise, and appreciation to the men of the 1st Brigade Combat Team for a job well done.

Signature Block

SSG Smith,
1. Please accept my thanks for volunteering your time in support of the Space and Missile Defense Command's 2009 Annual Awards Dinner.

2. The successful execution of this event was a direct result of your dedicated efforts and enthusiastic support.

3. Simply put, your support guaranteed the success of this important recognition ceremony. Thank you again for your selfless contributions.

Signature Block

SSG Smith,
1. Congratulations on your selection as the Maintenance Technician of the Month for April 2010. Your selection reflects the hard work and outstanding support you have given to the U.S. Army Garrison-Red Cloud's Directorate of Logistics and you can be justifiably proud.

2. In appreciation of your hard work, I'm awarding you a one-day pass. Please ensure you coordinate your time off with your supervisor.

3. Again, congratulations on your selection. It is my privilege to serve with motivated Soldiers such as yourself. Keep up the great work!

Sincerely,

Signature Block

Dear Staff Sergeant Smith,

Rarely in a career is a military professional called upon to respond to a vital contingency for which he is so confident and fully qualified. In every respect, the tiger team from the Engineer Battalion was ready for the challenge presented by the requirements of Operation ANVIL TREE. You and the other members of your extremely capable group of warriors did an absolutely outstanding job of securing the advanced position, setting up and establishing operations, and coordinating the movement of follow-on forces. Without your dedication to duty and tenacity under the extremely adverse conditions encountered, this operation would not have been the success that it was.

General Jones, the Task Force Commander, was extremely pleased with the results of your actions and spoke very highly of you and your unit. I know that successes like this are not automatic and are the result of long months of planning, practice, hard work, and sacrifice on the part of you and every member of your brigade. Thank you for your earnest support of our mission and the United States Army.

Signature Block

SUBJECT: Letter of Appreciation

1. I would like to express my sincere thanks for the excellent work of SSG John Smith. As a member of the Munitions Storage team, SSG Smith displayed great professionalism and technical expertise in transitioning from the storage, transfer, and implementation of conventional artillery munitions to the state-of-the-art, classified munitions complement. Working under stressful conditions and with little official guidance, his diligent efforts overcame numerous unforeseen obstacles and ensured a minimum amount of downtime.

2. SSG Smith assisted in developing procedures and policies for storage and use that corrected problems with compatibility issues and guaranteed the efficient integration into the Battalion's arsenal. The local instructions written by SSG Smith and his crew have been evaluated by several Field Artillery Battalions and adopted as standard operating procedure throughout U.S. Army Forces Command.

3. I want to express my sincere appreciation for SSG Smith's hard work and dedication in engineering this transition and ensuring the successful upgrade of our M270A1 MLRS capability. I also want to encourage him to continue to monitor and provide guidance and support to other units making the transition to advanced munitions. Our mission depends on the MLRS's abilities and that of capable young Soldiers like SSG Smith. Again, thanks for a job well done.

Certificate of Achievement

Commanders (or Command Sergeant Majors at the brigade level) may recognize periods of faithful service, and acts or achievements which do not meet the standards required for decorations by issuing DA Form 2442, Certificate of Achievement, or a Certificate of Achievement of local design to deserving members. These certificates are worth 5 points toward promotion. There is a maximum 20 points allowed for Certificates of Achievement.

IAW AR 600-8-22, Para 10-7, the following restrictions apply:

- Certificates of Achievement will be issued under such regulations as the local commander may prescribe.
- If a locally designed Certificate of Achievement is printed for use, it may bear reproductions of insignia. In the interest of economy, the use of color will be held to a minimum.
- The citation on such certificates will not be worded so that the act or service described appears to justify the award of a decoration.
- No distinguishing device is authorized for wear to indicate the receipt of a Certificate of Achievement.

In addition, AR 672-20, Incentive Awards, dictates:

Certificate of Achievement
a. The DA Form 2442 (Certificate of Achievement) may be granted by local commanders or other locally

authorized individuals as honorary recognition for individual or group contributions.
b. Eligibility will be determined by measuring contributions against the following example levels of achievement:
(1) Accomplished assigned duties in a commendable manner, demonstrating skill and initiative in either devising or improving work methods and procedures or both, causing a saving of manpower, time, space, or materials.
(2) Significantly improved employee morale and job performance.
(3) Demonstrated personal diligence or initiative which was directly responsible for meeting mission requirements or special workload projects involving unexpected difficulties and operational demands.

EXAMPLES

For completion of the Boot Strap Program while assigned to the 23M, Class of 214th FA, during the period 1 October 2008 through 20 December 2008. You have distinguished yourself by maintaining an 855 average throughout your training and participation in the Boot Strap Program. This accomplishment demonstrates the additional hard work, dedication to duty and outstanding soldierly qualities exemplified by the Boot Strap graduates. Your achievement reflects great credit upon yourself, your unit and the United States Army.

ꕤ

For achieving a first time go on all tasks tested during the phase III evaluation. This outstanding achievement demonstrates a high degree of initiative and dedication and reflects highly on you, your unit, and the United States Army. Keep up the good work!

ꕤ

For attaining a total score of 299 points on the army physical fitness test. The excellence you demonstrated in physical fitness is indicative of your hard work and determination to be a physically ready soldier. This achievement is significant and reflects great credit upon you, the 155th Combat Aviation Battalion and the United States Army. Army pride!

ꕤ

For exceptional achievement as NCOIC, Personnel Services, Headquarters Section, Redstone Arsenal, from 1 April 2009 to 10 July 2009. SSG Smith played a vital role in preparing the command for the Space and Missile Defense Command Awards Ceremony despite a shortage of personnel and support. He ensured all detachments were represented, deserving members were recognized and a strong unit participation. His efforts resulted in our most successful ceremony to date and reflect great credit upon him and the United States Army.

ꕥ

Effective 1 April 2010, you are hereby authorized to wear the 1st Infantry Division Combat Patch for wartime service. You have honorably served in the Iraq Theater of Operations as part of OPERATION IRAQI FREEDOM VII. Your sacrifice reflects great credit upon yourself, the 3rd Infantry Brigade Combat Team, the 1st Infantry Division and the United States Army.

Made in the USA
San Bernardino, CA
28 February 2014